MW00339829

WHAT YOUR COLLEAGUES ARE SAYING . . .

We know that every student is advancing their learning at a different speed. This book makes a great case for goal setting as a critical way to realize student potential. Chase Nordengren offers research-backed evidence along with valuable advice for all educators about the power of goal setting to advance learning, motivate students, and establish long-term knowledge that will help students succeed.

—Chris Minnich
Chief Executive Officer, NWEA

When students know the goals of learning, they are more receptive to teaching, feedback, and assessment and are more likely to engage and enjoy the hard work of learning. This is the go-to book to learn more about effective and efficient goal setting and how to involve the students in setting and evaluating progress to mastery and deeper learning goals. The book also recognizes that every student already has their goals; educators can learn how to work with these to entice them to also aim for their goals (and not the other way around).

—John Hattie
Author, *Visible Learning* series

As we find ourselves immersed in resetting and reimagining schools for student-directed learning, Chase Nordengren provides us with current research on student motivation while offering educators practical strategies for student goal setting. Through *Step Into Student Goal Setting*, practitioners are offered a well-grounded why for this practice along with essentials for measuring learning, supporting autonomy, developing a classroom culture of academic press, and one-on-one conversations, all of which empower learners as well as teachers on this journey. This is a tool that can be used by administrators with staff to shift the paradigm, by classroom teachers to reflect and rethink their positions on student-directed learning, and by schools to open the door to grounding themselves in how humans learn. Let's get started!

—Anna Sugarman
Professional Learning Coordinator, Shenendehowa Central Schools

Chase Nordengren's book carefully balances a grounding in research related to goal setting (with gentle reminders not to rely on a single study) with practical suggestions for how to turn that research into classroom practice. To support students in increasing their use of goal-setting practices and moving toward greater autonomy of learning, teachers may need to engage with similar strategies; to that end, Chase also provides opportunities for teachers to reflect, plan, and act on the recommendations within each chapter. This book provides a wealth of tools for teacher learning communities to engage with over an extended period of time to address an important teaching practice that will support student learning.

—Caroline Wylie
Principal Research Scientist, ETS

In his book, Chase Nordengren reminds us about the power of intentionality and how we can use goal-setting to empower our students to become agents in their own learning. With a combination of practical application and thoughtful approaches, he helps recast goal setting from an often-used strategy to a pedagogy that ensures the centering of our students. It's a perfect read for anyone who is ready to reignite purposeful learning.

—Sarah Brown Wessling
2010 National Teacher of the Year

What if the best parts of our assessment and teaching practices were focused on the humans they are intended to most impact? In other words, what if our assessment practices were student-centered by design? What if we could live these values in our classrooms, learn through empathy so we can understand the lived experience of each and every student, begin the learning journey by centering students as active partners, co-create aspirational outcomes, and liberate students to build their own pathways to achieve their visions? *Step Into Student Goal Setting* is an opportunity to do just that. Nordengren's book offers tangible steps that all educators and students can take as they unlearn disempowering educational habits and roles, opting instead for a student-powered system that elevates student involvement and shared decision making to give students a stake in their own future.

—Erin Whitlock
Professional Practice Consultant with the
Center for Great Public Schools at the Oregon Education Association

STEP INTO STUDENT
GOAL SETTING

STEP INTO STUDENT GOAL SETTING

A Path to Growth, Motivation, and Agency

Chase Nordengren

A Joint Publication

FOR INFORMATION:

Corwin

A SAGE Company

2455 Teller Road

Thousand Oaks, California 91320

(800) 233-9936

www.corwin.com

SAGE Publications Ltd.

1 Oliver's Yard

55 City Road

London EC1Y 1SP

United Kingdom

SAGE Publications India Pvt. Ltd.

B 1/I 1 Mohan Cooperative Industrial Area

Mathura Road, New Delhi 110 044

India

SAGE Publications Asia-Pacific Pte. Ltd.

18 Cross Street #10-10/11/12

China Square Central

Singapore 048423

President: Mike Soules

Associate Vice President and
    Editorial Director: Monica Eckman

Executive Editor: Tori Mello Bachman

Associate Content
    Development Editor: Sharon Wu

Editorial Assistant: Nancy Chung

Project Editor: Amy Schroller

Copy Editor: Erin Livingston

Typesetter: C&M Digitals (P) Ltd.

Proofreader: Dennis Webb

Cover Designer: Gail Buschman

Marketing Manager: Margaret O'Connor

Copyright © 2022 by Corwin Press, Inc.

All rights reserved. Except as permitted by U.S. copyright law, no part of this work may be reproduced or distributed in any form or by any means, or stored in a database or retrieval system, without permission in writing from the publisher.

When forms and sample documents appearing in this work are intended for reproduction, they will be marked as such. Reproduction of their use is authorized for educational use by educators, local school sites, and/or noncommercial or nonprofit entities that have purchased the book.

All third-party trademarks referenced or depicted herein are included solely for the purpose of illustration and are the property of their respective owners. Reference to these trademarks in no way indicates any relationship with, or endorsement by, the trademark owner.

Printed in Canada

Library of Congress Cataloging-in-Publication Data

Names: Nordengren, Chase, author.

Title: Step into student goal setting : a path to growth, motivation, and agency / Chase Nordengren.

Description: Thousand Oaks, California : Corwin | NWEA, [2022] | Series: Corwin Teaching Essentials | Includes bibliographical references and index.

Identifiers: LCCN 2021041374 | ISBN 9781071855201 (Paperback : acid-free paper) | ISBN 9781071858066 (ePub) | ISBN 9781071867082 (ePub) | ISBN 9781071867068 (PDF)

Subjects: LCSH: Motivation in education. | Goal (Psychology) | Effective teaching.

Classification: LCC LB1065 .N56 2022 | DDC 370.15/4–dc23/eng/20211106

LC record available at https://lccn.loc.gov/2021041374

This book is printed on acid-free paper.

22 23 24 25 26 10 9 8 7 6 5 4 3 2

DISCLAIMER: This book may direct you to access third-party content via Web links, QR codes, or other scannable technologies, which are provided for your reference by the author(s). Corwin makes no guarantee that such third-party content will be available for your use and encourages you to review the terms and conditions of such third-party content. Corwin takes no responsibility and assumes no liability for your use of any third-party content nor does Corwin approve, sponsor, endorse, verify, or certify such third-party content.

CONTENTS

PREFACE

We're at a moment of extraordinary reckoning in education.

In 2020 and 2021, a generational pandemic stressed nearly every aspect of our school systems, keeping students separated from the peers and resources that had supported their learning and forcing teachers to recreate the classroom in a foreign virtual environment. This period has required us to examine the cobwebbed corners of instructional practice and try to understand what about teaching and learning was essential, what could be skipped, and what was long overdue for a change. The pandemic has been hard on all students whose schools were closed but has been particularly hard on those with limited access to technology, home environments less conducive to studying, or the hardships and traumas of economic recession and personal illness. Crises often work as a magnifying glass: They enlarge the wicked problems that have always impacted students and bring into focus the challenges that have always confronted educators.

Even as this particular challenge continues, the questions it has raised point to areas where schooling in general needs to evolve. What does it mean to be in fifth grade, if every student experienced fourth grade differently? Are the grading systems that many thought were unfair and unreasonable during a pandemic fair and reasonable the rest of the time? How can the relationships among teachers, students, and learning change so that students can keep growing even if they are taught from a distance for weeks, months, or a year at a time? The next major disruption to learning—whether it comes in the form of a pandemic, a severe environmental event, economic migration, or something else we can't imagine yet—requires us to have better answers to those questions.

This book considers how goal setting for students contributes to those answers. By themselves, goals offer students the opportunity to take ownership over their learning, relate what they're studying to their long-term ambitions, and experience success regardless of how below or above grade level their current knowledge sits. What I hope you'll see in this book is the larger tapestry of effective teaching and learning practice that setting goals engages: from formative assessment practice to metacognition to social-emotional learning. These practices form the bedrock of an updated educational system prepared to deal with challenges like the pandemic, the increasing rate at which students transition between different schools and different school districts, and the difficult emotional pressures of growing up in the 21st century.

There are no silver bullets in education, no magic set of instructional or leadership techniques that produces above-average growth for all students at all times and under all circumstances. Setting goals isn't a silver bullet, either. What goal-setting practice provides is a framework linking practices of effective educators in ways that help better engage students with high-quality instruction. That framework is not an instant solution: It requires making choices about how to best use these practices, all meant to be made by the educators who know what students need best. Rather than dictating one path forward, this book hopes to highlight those choices and lead you through the process of making them.

ACKNOWLEDGMENTS

This book features the insights of nine current and former classroom teachers: Lindsay Deacon, Cara Holt, Eric Johnson, Matthew Marchoyok, Ryan McDermott, Caryn Miller, Alyssa Nestler, Courtney Pawol, and Erin Whitlock. My deepest thanks to them for the invaluable window they've opened into their practice. My colleagues at NWEA who supported this project are too many to name them all, but they include Erin Beard, Jennifer Morgan, Emily Vislocky, Vicki McCoy, and Jacob Bruno. Tori Bachman at Corwin and this book's peer reviewers provided essential feedback and support in bringing this project to fruition.

Along with magnifying wicked problems, periods such as these also highlight the strength, peace, and persistence we draw from those most important to us. That person for me is my wife, Hope, whose support and encouragement guided this book to its completion.

PUBLISHER'S ACKNOWLEDGMENTS

Corwin gratefully acknowledges the contributions of the following reviewers:

Melissa Wood Glusac
High School English Teacher
Thousand Oaks High School/CVUSD
Thousand Oaks, CA

Roshani Shah
Middle School Educator
Gwinnett County Public Schools
Suwanee, GA

ABOUT THE AUTHOR

Chase Nordengren, PhD, is a Senior Research Scientist at NWEA, where he supports the professional learning team with primary and secondary research that drives content innovation and instructional improvement. His work includes needs assessment and program evaluation services for partners, supporting school improvement processes, and thought leadership on formative assessment and student goal-setting practices. He received a PhD in Leadership, Policy, and Organizations in K-12 Systems from the University of Washington as a US Department of Education Institute of Educational Sciences (IES) predoctoral fellow.

INTRODUCTION

Two Revolutions in Learning

In our relentless drive toward improving learning for students, it's easy to forget just how far schools have come in the last few decades. Someone who hasn't been part of these changes would likely be surprised when walking into an average school. The neat rows of desks that screamed "classroom" thirty years ago aren't nearly as ubiquitous as they used to be. In schools with means, a single computer lab has been replaced by mobile devices or even a laptop assigned to each student. Students are exposed to a much wider literature canon and asked to wrestle with deep problems at earlier ages.

Despite all that progress, we know that there's still much to do in order to bring these types of innovations to every school that needs them. Few schools have the resources, the flexibility, or the expertise to apply every educational best practice with perfect fidelity. After conducting all the research and understanding what it means comes the often much more difficult task of understanding how to bring effective practices to all kinds of schools and adapt them to meet individual student needs. But the progress in education to date serves as an ideal point of reflection on how our ideas about students—and our systems for educating them—have changed.

Unlike past generations, we encourage our children to be both seen and heard. We ask teachers to mold them into active, critical, and happy individuals instead of simply compliant members of our community. Our students have their own heroes, their own dreams, and their own senses of right and wrong—and they're not afraid to tell us when their sense conflicts with ours.

Goal setting—the subject of this book—is about taking the spirit in which we educate and translating it into concrete instructional moves that can motivate students to learn more, express more confidence in themselves and their learning, and achieve their short- and long-term aspirations. It is first and foremost a creative and individualized practice, focusing on meeting our individual students where they are and

> Goal setting is about taking the spirit in which we educate and translating it into concrete instructional moves that can motivate students.

providing for their needs in the moment. And it serves as a link to some of the most important and innovative tools of effective instruction: formative assessment, student ownership, and social-emotional learning.

Both the history of educational progress and the research that has accompanied that history demonstrate why goal setting works in classrooms with all types of students. In the brief wander through that history that follows, what sticks out most are the ties researchers consistently find between students' academic learning and their social-emotional well-being. When schools serve students as people—and not as interchangeable widgets—they are both providing for students' emotional needs and delivering more effective instruction.

THE FIRST LEARNING REVOLUTION

In 2000, the National Research Council (part of the National Academies of Sciences) released the groundbreaking book, *How People Learn*. Developed and written over the course of two years by a committee including many of the leading lights in learning theory, child development, and psychology, the book captured rapid developments in how we understand thinking and learning. The proliferation of magnetic resonance imaging (MRI) technology in the 1980s and 1990s created never-before-seen pictures of brains at work. Neuroscience, in turn, began understanding how the brain is organized and how it functions—and how learning shapes it over time. Social science shifted as well; computer-assisted testing and automated scoring were used to compile large data sets about what students know and how they learned it. In the Council's words, these developments took learning "from speculation to science" (National Research Council, 2000, p. 3).

When added up, these developments and many others advanced a fundamentally new idea of how learning happens—from memorizing and repeating facts to building "the intellectual tools and learning strategies" that allow people to find and use information in their world (National Research Council, 2000, p. 5). To the 19th-century teacher in a one-room schoolhouse (and even to many 20th-century teachers), this constructivist approach to knowledge would be almost inconceivable: too hands-off, too varied, too chaotic. In the 21st century, it is an appropriate response not only to the increasing power of new research tools and techniques but also to a world that is constantly changing and evolving.

As our approach to learning changes, so do the goals of schooling. Gone (at least in theory) is the 19th- and 20th-century emphasis on efficiently cramming students' heads full of essential sets of facts and figures. In its place, schools are now asked to enable learners to identify problems, build solutions, and display the "adaptive expertise" required for new types of work and social engagement. To navigate this complex learning environment, school systems rely on standards: using learning statements to understand what students are expected to know and assessment to measure progress toward proficiency.

How People Learn updated several outmoded conceptions of how students learn. However, the reality portrayed in the report departs from ours in the relatively little attention it gives the cultures, contexts, and needs of individual learners. The most prominent learning studies highlighted in *How People Learn* were conducted in sterile labs rather than in classrooms, diminishing the importance of individual student differences. It would take another revolution to build a more complete conception of how learning works.

THE SECOND LEARNING REVOLUTION

In 2018, the National Academies of Sciences once again captured the contemporary landscape of learning science in *How People Learn II*. Working from the consensus of a similarly elite group of scholars, the second volume addresses remarkable developments in research examining learners, contexts, and cultures. Introducing new research methods and disciplines, this new text paints an updated picture of learning and of learners. "Learners function within complex developmental, cognitive, physical, social and cultural systems" that shape not only what people learn but also how they learn (National Academies of Sciences, Engineering, and Medicine, 2018, pp. 21-23). These systems impact learning at every stage, the authors write, and even change the biological development of the brain. "Culture fundamentally shapes all aspects of learning, from the wiring of the brain to the way that communities and societies organize learning activities" (p. 135).

How People Learn II merges a focus on the process of metacognition and executive function with a deeper understanding of the social systems in which learning takes place. "Motivation to learn is influenced by the multiple goals that individuals construct for themselves as a result of their life and school experiences and the sociocultural context in which learning takes place" (National Academies of Sciences, Engineering, and Medicine, 2018, p. 133). This context includes factors as diverse as a person's social identity, cross-cultural differences in perceptions of the self, safety and well-being in the home, and stereotype threat (the influence of prejudice and bias on a student's self-efficacy and self-esteem). Well-set personal goals, the definition suggests, are a student's pathway out of the adversity created by some of these factors.

Goals are an essential and recurring element of this new way of thinking. But *How People Learn II* approaches goals in a different way: Learning goals are individual, contextual, and constantly changing. Goals "are important for learning because they guide decisions about whether to expand effort and how to direct attention, foster planning, influence responses to failure, and promote other behaviors important to learning" (National Academies of Sciences, Engineering, and Medicine, 2018, p. 117). Goals are focused on what is meaningful and relevant to learners as they progress. The task of educators is to align teaching and learning to help students meet their goals.

> *Goals represent the path of learning from beginner to expert. But students don't all take a single path and aren't even all headed toward the same destination.*

What made goals suddenly so essential to learning? The answer lies in how these two revolutions come together. By 2000, research had conclusively demonstrated that students were individuals: Instructional strategies had to appeal to each student's unique needs and course of development to prepare the student for a world where critical thinking and adaptability had become central. By 2018, new research had enhanced that conclusion by illuminating the social forces, motivations, and contexts that make each student so different.

Goals represent the path of learning from beginner to expert. To embark on that journey, students must understand where they are going and how they will get there. Research shows that students don't all take a single path and aren't even all headed toward the same destination. Therefore, the process of charting their individual paths—goal setting—is a critical first step in the learning process for every student.

THE IMPACTS OF GOALS

Among effective instructional practices documented by researchers, goal setting is hiding in plain sight. While relatively few researchers have attempted to make a direct connection between goal-setting practices and improvements in students' standardized test scores, research literature is full of connections between achievement and key cultural factors affected by goal setting: student motivation, ownership of learning, and building an academic culture.

Education researcher John Hattie has been tracking the strongest influences on learning outcomes through his Visible Learning® framework since 2008. Hattie uses meta-analysis, a research tool that averages together impacts from several studies to find the overall effect of a type of intervention. These meta-analyses each focus on specific instructional and leadership strategies and the effect they have on student progress. Strategies that yield learning gains above the average effect size of 0.4 are identified as the most important opportunities for educators to impact student learning and improve schooling.

Hattie's (2021) review shows that setting appropriately challenging goals with clear goal intentions and high student commitment has positive and important impacts on student outcomes. Reviewing many of the other teaching strategies on Hattie's list shows why. Effective educators engage students in metacognition, through processes described as *cognitive task analysis, reflection, elaboration and organization,* and *evaluation and reflection.* They inspire students to try their hardest to learn (*effort, mastery learning*). And they provide regular feedback on what students are learning (*feedback, setting standards for self-judgment, providing formative evaluation*). Effective goal-setting techniques focus on providing students with all these benefits.

Among studies that do specifically examine goals and goal setting, Marzano (2009) finds an effect size between 0.42 and 1.37, representing a difference of between 18 and 41 percentile points for an individual student. Explanations for this impact come from how the studied programs influence metacognition, effort, and feedback cycles. Goal setting serves to cultivate student interest in learning and alter students' perceptions of their own abilities (Usher & Kober, 2012). Second, goal setting focuses students on specific outcomes and clarifies the relationship between those outcomes and success in the future (Stronge & Grant, 2014). Finally, goal setting contributes to an academic culture, explaining a significant portion of student achievement (Leithwood & Sun, 2018).

Changing a culture can feel abstract and impossible, but it doesn't have to. What we refer to as "school culture" comes down to what students think about learning: how learning works, what qualities good learners possess, and whether learning is worth their time and effort. Goal setting has the power to shape those attitudes for students and, in turn, shape the school culture around them.

The kinds of research captured by meta-analyses like Hattie's have a precision closer to an ax than a scalpel. It can't tell you precisely what to do in your classroom with your students: After all, the contexts and cultures of those learners play a big part in what works and what doesn't for them. What this research does do is direct our attention: It helps us identify which instructional practices can help us have the greatest impact on students and their learning, as long as those practices are done effectively and with consistent attention to individual learning needs.

THIS BOOK

This book is that scalpel, your guide to identifying an approach to helping your students set goals that works the best for them and for you. What's described here is not a program: There are no regimented schedules or scripts you must read word-for-word. For reasons that will hopefully become apparent, this is not a prescribed series of steps that must be followed in a certain way. Instead, this book offers a set of general principles that make goal setting successful and numerous examples from research and practice to support your own journey toward a goal-setting practice that's all your own.

The book's discussion is built on two pillars: evidence from published research and real-life examples from educators. The research featured here comes from a variety of focus areas in education—social-emotional learning, formative assessment, student ownership of learning, and student engagement—in which goal setting has emerged as a common topic of study and a source of immediate impact for students. The educators featured here represent a variety of grade levels and subject areas, all using their own version of a goal-setting practice to keep students motivated, interested, and working toward growth and deep learning. Throughout the book, I'll guide you through practical reflections and applications to jump-start your thinking and connect the general principles to your specific needs. I hope you'll treat both the research evidence and accounts of individual practice as relevant and important sources of information and inspiration to think about a goal-setting practice that fits the climate, culture, and context of your students and amplifies your own strengths as an educator.

We'll begin by exploring in depth the research on what makes a goal meaningful, attainable, and relevant for students. "Chapter 1: What Good Goals Look Like" focuses on three universal principles for all effective goals: that they are individual, that they focus students on mastery instead of performance, and that they are both meaningful and attainable. It connects the dots between the instructional power moves that goal setting enables to illustrate why the practice can be so powerful when implemented well.

The chapters that follow lay out five key principles around which to develop your goal-setting practice. "Chapter 2: Start Early and Keep It Up" focuses on how goals look with students in different grade levels and how they adjust with a student's cognitive development. Goal setting can start very early in a student's educational career—as early as the first week of kindergarten. The chapter examines how early practice with developmentally appropriate goals gives students the experience they need to excel at goal setting in later grades.

"Chapter 3: Build the Habit" explores how to make goal setting a routine part of your classroom practice, including tracking progress and updating goals over time. The central element of any good goal-setting practice is one-on-one conversations with students, reviewing what they know and setting the path for what they're ready to learn next. The chapter describes the necessary elements of those conversations and provides several example protocols to use with students to help them think through their goals.

"Chapter 4: Showcase Success Through Balanced Assessment" builds on goal-setting conversations, showing how educators can amplify the impact of goals by providing students with ample opportunities to witness their own growth and that of their peers. The chapter looks at the role of frequent formative assessment in enriching goal conversations with concrete opportunities for students to demonstrate their learning. It also explores the use of personal best goals as an alternative motivator to keep students focused on mastery.

"Chapter 5: Create Personal Relevance" centers relevance as an essential aspect of goals that students truly own. The chapter considers how teachers can connect goals to students' interests, aspirations, and motivators. It explores a set of practices for focusing on students' long-term learning intentions that can help provide underlying relevance to a host of classroom activities.

"Chapter 6: Use Student Choice to Support Autonomy" describes how setting and meeting goals can empower students and deepen their learning. The chapter summarizes extensive research on the connection between student goals and student ownership of learning. It also describes in depth how to balance student autonomy with directive coaching appropriate to each student's current level of independence, ensuring that goals are both meaningful and realistic.

The book concludes with a clear call to action for you to build a goal-setting practice, based on this evidence, that adapts to the unique contexts and needs of your classroom.

A NEW KIND OF TEACHING

If you're like most teachers, you received little formal training in how to use data to plan learning with students (Jimerson, 2016). Chances are good that you picked up this book to meet one of your own goals: You want to drive growth for your students, close achievement gaps, or make time and space in your classroom for student voice and choice. These goals are important to consider in building your strategy; they're also a great way of connecting with your students. Seeing teachers set and meet their own goals—whether professional or personal—shows that this process isn't busy work but instead is part and parcel of building a successful life. From the first week of kindergarten, students can begin immersing themselves in a culture where everyone sets goals, monitors their progress, and celebrates their success.

It's my hope that you also see in this book a different way of thinking about teaching. The "sage on the stage" notion that characterized teacher training for much of the 20th century not only runs counter to the best interests of students, but it is also hopelessly impractical. Anyone who has been in a classroom in the last decade knows the diversity of learning strengths and needs represented there. While these needs have, as of this writing, been exacerbated by interrupted learning caused by the COVID-19 pandemic, they were always there.

This book considers teaching not as delivering from a stage but as directing learning. As the learning director, your job is to connect your students with the content, techniques, and motivation they need to be successful learners. While that task is formidable, the rewards are immense: helping mold individual students using the materials and activities that are best for them. Goal setting is the glue that binds those activities together.

WHAT GOOD GOALS LOOK LIKE

Student goal setting is one of the most consequential strategies available for teachers to drive improvements in student outcomes. Marzano (2009) finds that goal setting can produce student learning gains between 18 and 41 percentile points. *Visible Learning*, Hattie's (2013) seminal review of the evidence behind effective learning, cites setting concrete goals—alongside formative evaluation, student feedback, mastery learning, and metacognition—as teaching strategies with the clearest positive impacts on student outcomes. Further, Hattie identifies student social-emotional competencies, including motivation, persistence, and reduced anxiety as substantial contributions by students to their overall academic success. A well-executed goal setting strategy can enable each of these factors.

Student goal setting is powerful because it connects students to some significant instructional power moves.

Student goal setting is powerful because it connects students to some significant instructional power moves: formative assessment, providing feedback, improving motivation, and building an academic culture. Goal setting helps students focus on specific outcomes, encourages them to challenge themselves, and clarifies the connection between an immediate activity and future results (Stronge & Grant, 2014). Goal setting can help students build competence, establish control or autonomy, cultivate their interest in learning, and alter their perceptions of their own abilities (Usher & Kober, 2012). Far from being set in stone, such abilities are malleable—and you can shape them by helping students set their own goals.

Goal setting is a form of student-involved data use (Jimerson, 2016), putting students right at the center of processes, including reviewing data, monitoring progress, and reflecting to inform learning. Research in this area shows that goals crafted in the right way can maximize learning opportunities. This chapter surveys foundational research on student goal setting to understand what kinds of goals best promote student engagement, persistence, motivation, and achievement.

WHAT KINDS OF GOALS WORK?

Beyond the classroom, goals have become a ubiquitous tool to motivate and change behaviors, and examples of their impact on our culture abound. Fitness trackers and smart watches (what the tech industry calls "wearables") are wildly popular: A quarter of U.S. adults used a wearable device monthly in 2019, and around 4 million new users start using wearables each year (Wurmser, 2019). Among other features, these devices set a goal for the number of steps their users take each day and track progress against that goal. Increasing the number of steps you take daily is associated with a number of positive health outcomes, from better sleep quality and joint mobility to improved brain health and lower risk of heart disease. Examining how we make goals related to our steps illustrates not only the potential of goals to change individual behaviors but also the pitfalls of goals that are set with too little context in mind.

Most fitness trackers start with the same goal for all walkers: 10,000 steps a day. While the origins of this target number aren't fully known, epidemiologist I-Min Lee suggests that it came from a 1965 product by Japanese manufacturer Yamasa Clock. They called their pedometer *Manpo-kei*, or "10,000 steps meter," likely because the kanji character for 10,000 looks like a person walking (see Figure 1.1; Maldarelli, 2020). This easy-to-remember goal may have sold pedometers, but it wasn't based in science.

Effective marketing has convinced many of us that walking 10,000 steps is the key to good health for everyone. The full story, not surprisingly, is a bit more complicated. Lee's work suggests that older women

Figure 1.1

Source: Glyphwiki

experience improved health outcomes starting around 4,400 steps a day, with limited added benefit above 7,500 steps a day (Lee et al., 2019). Fitness tracker manufacturer Fitbit recommends different step counts depending on your fitness goals, some well below 10,000 steps and some well above (Rosenbaum, 2019). If the goal is only to motivate the user to make healthier choices, their specific number of steps may not matter at all (Giddens et al., 2017). Beyond these caveats, building lifelong fitness requires greater context than the ability to hit an arbitrary milestone. By themselves, wearables cannot overcome a lack of spaces or equipment for exercise or not having specific planned activities to help individuals reach their step goals (Sullivan & Lachman, 2016).

The literal steps we take each day are a perfect analogy for the steps of learning each student takes. As with a person's step count, every student starts their learning journey from a different place. Each student responds to different incentives and motivators for learning. And students also need help eliminating barriers to learning progress: making sure they have the learning spaces, the content, and the context to achieve their highest potential. Because of these factors, setting the same short-term goals for each student doesn't make sense. To ensure educational equity, the destination of every student's learning journey should be the same: the knowledge and skills required to live and work as an empowered, engaged, and competent member of their community. But although that destination is common, the paths students will take to get there look very different.

This common form of goal-setting behavior is a reminder that goals, by themselves, aren't magical. When setting learning goals, teachers and students need to consider the factors that make goals effective and design goals that support specific and long-term changes in behaviors and mindsets. Effective goals have three primary characteristics:

- **Effective goals are individualized.** While the ultimate destination is the same for all learners, the routes they take to get there can vary greatly depending on students' current status, academic areas of strengths and weakness, motivation, and resources available to them. Allowing learners to choose their goals themselves is the best path toward ensuring that goals are right for them.

- **Effective goals support mastery over performance.** While we're all motivated by different factors, research shows that goals focused on individual improvement produce better outcomes than focusing on appearing competent or outperforming others (Anderman et al., 2011; Ciani et al., 2010; Maehr & Zusho, 2009). Effective goals tap into the authentic drives of individual learners.

▶ **Effective goals balance what is meaningful with what is attainable.** Just as 10,000 steps may not be reasonable for someone just starting out, a student several grade levels behind may not be ready to achieve grade-level mastery in one school year. Effective short-term goals keep the ultimate goal of proficiency in mind while establishing milestones that allow students to feel successful and empowered along the way.

Finally, the best goals incorporate opportunities for support and motivation along the way. The rest of this book provides concrete tips and strategies to support students through their own process of setting, working toward, and celebrating their learning goals.

GOALS ARE INDIVIDUALIZED

The heart of an effective goal-setting process lies in the students themselves. Whether we choose to acknowledge it or not, students are ultimately responsible for when, where, and how they will learn. While a teacher can never force students to apply themselves to the task of learning, there are many tools at the teacher's disposal to motivate and engage students in the hard work of learning. Goal setting brings these tools together into practice.

Class- or grade-level goals can play an important role in an overall goal-setting strategy, especially around social-emotional or behavioral objectives. Many students are motivated, for example, by the opportunity to support their team (the class) as it meets a collective goal to read independently for a certain amount of time or keep a high attendance rate. These can also be great techniques for introducing students to the processes around goal setting, especially at younger ages.

But when it comes to learning targets and objectives, no two students start from the same place. Further, the best path for a student from their starting place to the ultimate goal may look very different. That's why student learning is most directly impacted where teachers and students collaborate on goals that start from what they know today and focus on a target that is both reasonable and ambitious for them.

There's no doubt that setting individual goals for students is a big undertaking. There are, however, a few general principles guiding the process:

1. **Start with assessment data:** When we sit down to plan a journey, whether a hike through the woods or a drive across the country, we start with two pieces of information: where we are

and where we want to go. We figure out where students are by using assessments: formative and summative experiences that help us understand what students have learned and what they are ready to learn next. When identifying a student's individual goal, assessment data can be a big help. Data from standardized assessments, for instance, can show a student's achievement level relative to peers and how their future achievement level might compare at the end of the year. By using formative assessment, teachers can dive deep into student knowledge in a particular area of mastery, identify key misconceptions, and make targeting those misconceptions central to the journey (Heritage, 2010). Chapter 4 goes into more detail on how to use assessments as part of a goal-setting process.

2. **Look toward mastery but understand how the path may shift:** The end of the journey is a point we plot for all students: mastery, whether learning key content, grasping an academic construct, or meeting grade-level standards. Focusing our educational system on cultivating learners requires us to be clear about what students need to know to be successful in postsecondary education, a career, and their civic life. Setting our aspirations high is a key component of equity, ensuring that all students are given the opportunity to achieve at the highest potential. But focusing all attention on that goal for all students may be less helpful for those students who grow differently from the average learner. Setting the same educational goal for every student doesn't make sense, because they're all starting from different places. Further, effective goals address not only a student's past and future performance but also their abilities, motivations, and available resources. Effective goals require keeping the ambitions of mastery in check with what's realistic and reasonable for individual students.

3. **Keep goals short term:** The key to balancing our ultimate goal of mastery with realism is setting frequently updated short-term goals, providing ample opportunity for students to celebrate as their learning improves. Short-term goals allow teachers to take advantage of what they know about students—their areas of strength, their interests, and their motivations—to organize learning in the way that best maintains the students' energy toward a learning objective. Short-term goals should also support adapting instruction for students who are above grade level. These students can further their learning both by engaging in more complex tasks on grade-level content and by working with content above their grade level; the right mix of these

practices is different for every student. Goal setting provides an opportunity to set a path through accelerated content that maintains high expectations while keeping students' learning grounded in meaning.

4. **Balance choice with support:** As Chapter 6 describes in detail, goals are only individualized when students make real choices about their goals. Motivated and supported learners choose their own goals, understand what their goals mean, and play a central role in building the plan to achieve those goals. Research discussed in that chapter shows clear benefits associated with helping students take ownership of the direction and focus of their learning. But just as students are poorly served by having their goals dictated from on high, they are also left ill prepared if they have to make every choice on their own without fully understanding what they have learned, what they need to learn next, and what resources are available to them to support that learning. Different students need different levels of support, depending on their age, maturity level, personality, and other factors. What matters most is making sure the final choice of a goal is the student's, even if that choice is made from options the teacher has designed.

> *Goal setting provides an opportunity to set a path through accelerated content that maintains high expectations while keeping students' learning grounded in meaning.*

These four ideas—all focused on how goals can be made relevant, meaningful, and appropriate to individual learners—are the animating force behind a goal-setting process that students are genuinely invested and interested in. Like any other good instructional practice, goal setting can easily become a form of compliance, another form in a sea of busy work that teachers ask students to complete. By demonstrating your interest in a student's individual success, you extend to them an invitation to think about their learning and craft a plan that will help them be successful.

GOALS SUPPORT MASTERY

Educators know that "teaching to the test"—focusing instruction only on the set of knowledge or skills a particular assessment measures—leads to an incomplete and superficial understanding of academic content. For the same reason, students should avoid pursuing goals focused exclusively on maximizing performance on an assessment—in other words, goals that set students up for "learning to the test."

What students have in mind when they set goals is as important as the goals themselves.

Teachers have substantial influence over how students perceive goals—even more than their parents or other adults (National Academies of Sciences, Engineering, and Medicine, 2018). Just as students' attitude toward learning will play a major role in the goals they set for themselves, so too can guidance toward the right kinds of goals influence attitudes by offering a picture of what good learning looks like.

Research shows that people have two different types of mindsets about their goals—mastery and performance—and which mindset they choose often dictates whether they will succeed at meeting their goals.

THE RESEARCH ON MASTERY AND PERFORMANCE GOALS

Mastery goals are those goals that focus on increasing the goal setter's competence or understanding of a subject (National Academies of Sciences, Engineering, and Medicine, 2018). Mastery is what students are looking for when they want to learn in order to get better at something or become a more well-rounded person. The motivation to complete a mastery goal is intrinsic—that is, internal to the goal setter.

Performance goals are those goals that focus on helping the learner appear competent or outperform others (National Academies of Sciences, Engineering, and Medicine, 2018). When students are focused on their grades, their class rank, or pleasing others, they're not focused on learning for learning's sake. Students whose goal is solely a top rank or a passing grade undermine the value of in-depth knowledge of a subject that supports longer-term learning.

Several studies have found a negative orientation between performance goals and student outcomes (Anderman et al., 2011; Ciani et al., 2010; Maehr & Zusho, 2009). Why might this be? Scholars of student motivation suggest that all goals create a program of learning for the student, bringing with it different actions to perform, different decisions about when to keep up or reduce effort, and different consequences for meeting or falling short of expectations. "Each goal, in a sense, creates and organizes its own world—each evoking different thoughts and emotions and calling forth different behaviors" (Elliott & Dweck, 1988, p. 11).

Performance orientations set up an environment that is antithetical to successful learning. A performance orientation may cause a student to give up too soon (after building only a limited understanding of a content area) or, alternatively, push the student to meet an impossible standard (Ciani et al., 2010). It may also introduce a slate of negative emotions to the learning process, including anxiety, fear of failure, and self-doubt (Ames & Archer, 1988). Students with performance orientations may not seek help for fear that their question will show what they don't know. These mindsets work against the pursuit of deep mastery.

Mastery orientations jump-start motivation and student ownership of learning.

Conversely, mastery orientations jump-start motivation and student ownership of learning. Across three studies, students who focused on mastery looked forward to new challenges, expended more effort, engaged in deep processing, and felt more in control of their own learning (McGregor & Elliot, 2002). Other studies have found that students who see their classes as mastery focused enjoy class more and use more strategies for self-regulation (Wolters, 2004). Over time, the use of mastery-oriented goals can even overcome deficit mindsets originating from students' prior life experiences (Ames, 1992; Ames & Archer, 1988). The correspondence between student orientation and classroom orientation also matters: Students predisposed to mastery orientations who found themselves in performance-oriented classrooms tended to show lower effort (Wolters, 2004).

Admittedly, the news on performance goals is not all bad: Some studies have found potential benefits to student learning based in performance orientations, particularly in short-term activities (Maehr & Zusho, 2009). To understand these differences, Martin Maehr and Akane Zusho suggest that there are really two kinds of performance goals: ones based in healthy competition with peers and ones focused on avoiding the appearance of failure. Goals in which students aspire to high performance have better impacts than those in which students fear low performance (McGregor & Elliot, 2002).

Intuitively, there may be times and places where offering a little competition makes sense. There's no reason, for example, to stop offering game-based learning activities in class as one tool in a basket of engaging formative assessment strategies. Evidence suggests, however, that the context of these activities and the messages they communicate about teaching and learning are critical to keeping their impact positive (Ames & Archer, 1988; Cauley & McMillan, 2010). Even in a competitive environment, it's up to teachers to give students permission to hesitate, get the answer wrong, or correct themselves. The learning is the point. Unequivocally, Maehr and Zusho (2009) write, performance goals about avoiding failure hurt learning.

Ultimately, we all want students to value learning for its own sake, make an effort because they choose to, and avoid the kinds of thinking that lead to deficit mindsets. As this book will repeatedly emphasize, practicing goal setting with students is not only about helping them meet a specific goal, it also trains students in how and why they should set goals throughout their lives.

REFLECT

Identify a student in your class and imagine two goals for the student: one with a mastery orientation and one with a performance orientation. Consider how focusing on each might impact what that student does in your classroom and how they reflect on their own learning.

MAKING A SHIFT TO MASTERY GOALS

The good news is that teaching strategies can guide students toward a mastery orientation and away from some of the worst pitfalls of performance goals. These opportunities come when teachers lead students in exploring data. In a 2014 study, Marsh, Farrell, and Bertrand interviewed teachers and leaders in six middle schools on how they framed data conversations with students. By matching these sources of evidence, they were able to understand the relationship between the instruction that leaders encouraged, teacher classroom moves, and attitudes about goals.

The majority of teachers who were followed in this study applied performance orientations. These teachers focused on communicating student status on assessments by posting the names of students scoring *proficient* or *advanced* on a data wall. Both in conversations with students and in conversations with other teachers, these teachers compared the performance of students to each other. Parties and prizes were provided to students who got high scores on assessments. Most importantly, students had little involvement in the process of interpreting, understanding, and acting on the results of their assessments.

Data displays in schools have become a ubiquitous feature of the teacher's lounge and classroom alike. There's nothing inherently flawed about these kinds of visuals. As with goals themselves, however, the motivations behind these displays matter. A visualization that makes private results public—and implicitly shames students who didn't make the mark—will likely encourage competition at the expense of mastery. Visuals that depict the growth of the whole class can have the opposite effect, uniting students in celebrating their common successes.

Teachers in the study who were instead driven by a mastery orientation saw higher levels of student engagement in the process of understanding their data. Those teachers used practices that were consistently focused on growth. Individual student data was shared privately and discussed in the context of student performance relative to standards rather than to other students. Teachers rewarded effort and progress rather than absolute achievement and students worked together analyzing misconceptions and correcting previous work to build collective understanding of content.

Students who are focused on a performance goal may also miss important steps in learning the essential content contained within the standards (and ideally within their learning goals). Mastery goals are beneficial because they provide students with the opportunity to reflect on their learning by deconstructing abstract standards into meaningful learning targets using student-friendly language. Teachers can use their own understanding of the standards, combined with learning progressions and other tools, to guide students in the process of breaking standards down into appropriate goals. For students striving to master something, understanding what will be mastered is the first step toward articulating a goal for mastering it. Performance goals skip this valuable step; students can be so focused on achieving top marks that they lack introspection on the connection between the content on a particular test and the broader scope of learning in that content area.

Using mastery-oriented behaviors in the classroom encourages three big mindset shifts for students. According to Good and Lavigne (2017), mastery-oriented students share the following characteristics:

- **Efficacy.** Students are confident they can succeed at their goal if they put in reasonable effort.

- **Ownership of success.** Students attribute success to their own ability and effort while not blaming their abilities for their failures.

- **Growth mindset.** Students believe academic ability can change and improve through learning, which motivates them to continue trying when work gets challenging or if they experience initial setbacks.

Especially as students are first adapting to goal setting, they may have several important reasons for identifying performance-oriented goals: wanting to avoid punishment, merit praise, or satisfy a competitive urge. These initial reasons for setting a particular goal may conceal a deeper motivation. We are all, understandably, interested in being able to succeed in the world around us. Underlying both mastery and performance orientations is the desire all students have for competence and success (Maehr & Zusho, 2009). Part of the learning process for students originally invested in performance-oriented goals is learning how true success is achieved: through consistent hard work.

As you reflect on experiences with setting student goals in the past, you may remember times when goals appeared to backfire, introducing a competitive and reductionist view of learning to the classroom. A performance orientation is likely to blame for some of those negative outcomes. Focusing on mastery is one part of goal setting that must be in place in order for goals to work effectively.

 **PLAN**

Pick a content standard at your grade level and consider how that standard could be introduced into a mastery goal for a particular student. How would you guide the student toward reframing that content standard in their own words? Plan a conversation with this student that would help direct them toward a focus on mastery.

GOALS ARE MEANINGFUL AND ATTAINABLE

Completing a goal—any goal—requires persistence. When learning to cook, few people come right out of the gate making delicious, mistake-free meals. Instead, becoming better at cooking means enduring a lot of cut fingers and inedible dishes in the process of becoming the chef you want to be. To make an omelet, you have to break some eggs—and to learn to make a delicious omelet, prepare to break a hundred more.

The good news is that persistence as a trait is malleable; it can change and improve based on the experiences that students have in school (Wolters, 2004). Goal setting is one of those key experiences. However, student persistence is not strengthened by just any type of goal. To keep students motivated, goals must balance two important priorities: meaning for the student and attainability based on the student's current status.

These two objectives sometimes find themselves in tension with each other, as more meaningful goals may also be more difficult to attain. Still, there is an innate desire to want to move beyond goals that are easily obtainable; no aspiring cook wants to be stuck making grilled cheese sandwiches forever! Fortunately, every completed basic dish and every new technique or process is another stepping-stone that propels the amateur chef to achieve more and more prowess. Goal setting provides the opportunity to break the journey toward mastering a skill into steps that are easy to understand as well as multiple opportunities to celebrate success.

Questions of meaning are at the heart of the two questions students are always asking their teachers: "Why do I need to know this?" and "When will I use this in real life?" While younger students may not pose questions quite this way, keeping all students engaged requires a clear connection between the day's learning and how students can accomplish something, feel prepared for something, or have fun. Why, after all, would any of us want to learn if that learning didn't reward us in return?

Meaningful goals are a concrete clue to a learner's identity: They highlight why the learner wants to learn and connect the lesson of the day or week to an overall set of knowledge and skills that will help the learner build a meaningful life (Husman & Lens, 1999). Chapter 5 shares several concrete techniques for uncovering what drives learners and helping them build that understanding into goals.

Making those techniques work well requires a deep understanding of content: what students know now, what they're getting ready to learn next, and the connections between those skills. For students embarking on learning new content, it may not be easy to comprehend how studying plot archetypes will support their dream to become a writer or how understanding surface area sets them on a path to being a great architect. But what we call "college and career readiness" isn't merely the purview of high school teachers: It's the sum of what students learn throughout their educational career.

Effective goals must also be **attainable** by students. Imagine beginning your culinary education by undertaking a gourmet, multicourse dinner. The struggle to complete the meal successfully—and the sting when it doesn't turn out quite as you'd hoped—would likely discourage you from ever wanting to cook again. The role of teachers is to provide students with the information and context necessary to understand what is realistically achievable in a given amount of time with a given level of experience.

Focusing on attainability in the short term does not mean limiting a student's horizons in the long term. Underlying all goal-setting practice is the belief that all students are capable of achieving at high levels, given the right combination of motivations and supports. Frequent goal conversations, discussed in Chapter 3, will help provide opportunities to regularly reconsider a student's growth trajectory and adjust the rigor of their goals accordingly.

When striking a balance between what is meaningful and what is attainable in a goal, there are no easy answers. An ostensibly out-of-reach goal can be more in reach if that goal is meaningful to the student. Evidence suggests that when motivated, students will aspire to meet harder goals and will achieve more over time (Ames, 1992; Cauley & McMillan, 2010; Seifert, 2004; Wolters, 2004). Gathering as much data as you can through assessment and considering those data alongside the needs and strengths of an individual student will give you the best chance to steer their goal in the right direction.

 ACT

How can you connect a learning target achieved at this developmental level with goals and aspirations that are more long term? With the features of high-quality goals in mind, fill out the goal-setting template in Figure 1.2. After finishing the book, you'll return to this reflection and note any major shifts in your opinions, perspectives, or the tactics you intend to use when setting goals with students.

Figure 1.2 Goal Setting and Action Planning at the Student Level

1. How do you set goals for a student? How do you determine each goal?

   _____

   _____

2. What resources are needed to accomplish the goal?

   _____

   _____

3. What resources could help when discussing goal setting with students and parents?

   _____

   _____

4. What will make this learning evidence meaningful?

   _____

   _____

5. What will a student need to learn in order to meet his or her goal?

   _____

   _____

6. Where will you find information about areas of strength and stretch?

   _____

   _____

7. How will you use this information about each student when planning instruction?

   _____

   _____

8. How will you involve the student in setting their goals?

   _____

   _____

SUPPORTING GOALS THAT LEAD TO GROWTH

Goal setting is a process that is "co-regulated," determined through the joint work of students and teachers. Goals happen at the intersection of a student's own social-emotional regulation, the structures of their learning situation and environment, the direct interventions of their teacher, and the tools the teacher uses for instruction and assessment (Allal, 2020). Effective goals are individually tailored to students, focus on mastery instead of performance, and balance meaningfulness with attainability. But this foundation can be shaky without the steadfast support of the student's teacher as mentor, coach, and learning guide.

A positive learning culture is the sum of individual actions, including correctly framing data conversations, providing positive public feedback, and creating opportunities to reflect on learning. Moving forward, this book will address some of the key decisions in curriculum, instruction, and assessment that teachers can make to support a goal-setting process that motivates learners, empowers them to own the learning process, and drives higher achievement. Examples from practicing educators lead the way, not as a specific prescription for how to do goal setting in a particular way but as sources of inspiration and a way to ground abstract principles in concrete practice. The following chapters also contain ample opportunities to reflect, plan, and act on your own goal-setting strategy attuned to your particular students.

As you continue, consider what it will take for you to set (and attain) your own goal of implementing student goal setting as a routine and central element of your teaching practice. Just as I don't know the right number of steps you should walk each day to support your fitness goals, I don't know the precise sequence of steps you should take to make goal setting a meaningful and actionable part of your instruction. Instead, look for the research-based strategies, motivation, support, and context that will help you determine the goal-setting strategy that will work best for your students—and for you.

CHAPTER SUMMARY

> Effective goals are individualized: They let learners choose the targets and pathways that make the most sense for them.

▶ Effective goals support a mastery orientation over a performance orientation, focusing on how the goal setter can increase their understanding in a subject rather than focusing on how to compete with others or meet an arbitrary bar. Teachers play a central role in leading students to mastery orientations by how they communicate the purpose of learning tasks, show student results, and reward effort and progress.

▶ Effective goals are both meaningful and attainable, providing ambitious opportunities for students to show growth while also taking into account what is realistic, given where students are starting from.

START EARLY AND KEEP IT UP

Setting Goals for All Students

When kids start school, they also begin in earnest the long process of becoming who they want to be. They develop likes and dislikes, make friends (and hopefully not enemies), and begin to think about the things they want to do with their lives. Of course, we know these ideas will change: Rare is the aspiring five-year-old astronaut who keeps that ambition going in the long term. But learning the types of things students want to know, do, and be still provides a valuable opportunity to link their academic growth to their identities as human beings.

In education circles, we often hear about goals for secondary students in the context of the barrage of career decisions, college applications, and other choices they are making about how to begin their adult lives. These goals are incredibly important. When students have made the decision about what college they want to go to or which career they want to pursue, setting meaningful and realistic academic goals is a great tool to help them understand the knowledge and skills they'll need to achieve those particular ambitions.

But while high school is where students often start to make plans to realize their dreams, they begin dreaming long before that. Goals can keep students of any age motivated and accelerate their learning.

🗨 USING GOALS AS STEPPINGSTONES

Courtney Pawol, a first-grade teacher with a deep focus on building resilience and growth mindset in students, is enthusiastic about the use of goal setting in her classroom. She's found that students' aspirations, even at a young age, can be the source of goals that drive academic growth as they build habits of mind for students. She described for me how carefully layering student choice with more direct guidance can help students narrow in on their goals:

> I say, "What's your goal in reading?" That's a huge question for a first grader, and they will usually say something like, "I want to read *Harry Potter*." Well, some first graders can read *Harry Potter*, but that's not a very attainable goal. . . . You have to guide them by asking, "What are you going to do to achieve that goal? What's going to help you read *Harry Potter*?" (Pawol, personal communication)

In this way, teachers can use an aspiration to motivate students to focus on concrete, grade-appropriate learning objectives that provide a stepping-stone to the more ambitious end goal.

As a process, goal setting is about helping students harness their aspirations and frame them in the shorter term to support the students' academic growth. As early as the first week of kindergarten, teachers can talk to students about what they want to do, who they want to be, and how academic growth will help them get there. Even if those early goals are small, and even if students don't succeed at first, starting the process of working with goals early prepares them to make it a regular and ordinary part of their education.

THE RESEARCH ON ACADEMIC CULTURE

Likely, you haven't achieved every single goal you set out for yourself in your lifetime—maybe a goal was too ambitious or you gave yourself too little time to get it done or you didn't have the resources you needed to see it through. Even if you fell short of achieving the goal, you likely learned something about how to set goals next time from the experience. You also got to keep all of the learning and growth you achieved along the way, despite not hitting your ultimate target.

The process of setting goals, whether it ends in success or failure, teaches students how learning works. By interacting with their goals, students learn that effort is rewarded, that learning happens over time, and that the best response to falling off the path is to get back up again. Especially in the younger grades, students still have a lot to learn about how to set the best goals for themselves. But with deliberate cultivation, teachers can use goal setting to create a context—a culture—in which students learn how to learn.

> By interacting with their goals, students learn that effort is rewarded, that learning happens over time, and that the best response to falling off the path is to get back up again.

ACADEMIC PRESS

The research of Leithwood and Sun (2018) has provided important insights into what makes up a supportive and productive academic culture. Leithwood and Sun name academic press as a vital component of academic culture, alongside a supportive disciplinary environment and using instructional time well. Academic press connects academic goals of all types with the kinds of supports students need to make the goals reasonable.

Academic press includes three key ideas:

1. Setting goals that are both ambitious and reasonable

2. Cultivating a positive response from students to those goals

3. Providing leadership supports for achieving goals

The research on academic press demonstrates the key role goals play in the kinds of academic cultures that support and promote student achievement. Consider the elementary language arts teacher focused on building a strong academic press for her students. That culture starts with her words: She makes clear that all students are expected to take on challenging reading tasks that expand their comprehension and interpretation skills. She supports that expectation by providing students with rigorous texts tuned both to their reading abilities and their individual interests. Her students respond to the confidence and trust she has given them by getting excited about achieving their individual goals, eagerly taking on new challenges, and not getting discouraged when they occasionally get sidetracked. Her principal sees this success and supports her academic press in big ways (providing curricular resources and the freedom to differentiate instruction for students) and small ones (throwing a pizza party each quarter for students who make their goals). What students experience is an environment in which every adult and all their peers believe in their ability to succeed and do whatever they can to support that success.

Critically, academic press is positively associated with student achievement in all types of schools, at all grade levels, and for all types of students. Leithwood and Sun's (2018) work, focused on Canadian elementary school teachers, showed a positive relationship between academic press and improved scores on standardized assessments. Other studies they cite support the use of academic press as students grow older. Anderman et al. (2011) found similar impacts among high school teachers in multiple subjects who accompanied academic press with instructional scaffolding and a focus on building rapport with their students.

AUTONOMY SUPPORT

Students are empowered in an academic culture when they are provided with autonomy support, which requires providing students with as much choice as possible within a given situation (Ciani et al., 2010). Note the caveat there: *as much choice as possible.* Obviously, a first or second grader might not be as independent in selecting a goal as an older student. However, teachers can consider a student's perspectives, aspirations, approaches to learning, and strengths when suggesting a goal to them.

Supporting autonomy is the most straightforward way teachers can put an emphasis on mastery goals in the classroom. By bringing examples of a mastery orientation into the classroom and giving students the freedom to apply those examples to their own work, teachers provide hands-on experience in how to pursue learning for the right reasons. "Teachers whose students reported more instructional and motivational support communicated an emphasis on building understanding, and demonstrated that being unsure, learning from mistakes, and seeking help are inevitable parts of learning" (Anderman et al., 2011, p. 174).

Modeling this level of choice for students can even provide a buffer against students pursuing goals for the wrong reasons (Ciani et al., 2010). Students have a variety of influences on how they think about school. The performance orientations described in the last chapter are pushed in all sorts of places in our culture, among students' peers, and even in their families. Still, teachers have the power to counter these influences by leaving the door open to student choice. Giving students the opportunity to pursue their own learning path allows them to discover for themselves the orientation toward learning that will make them feel the most successful.

Many students are afraid that making mistakes on a particular assignment or quiz will forever prevent them from achieving at a high level. Based on their past experiences, for example, a student may come into a math class intently focused on making the highest grades they can. In a goal-setting conversation, a teacher can use questions to reveal some of these mindsets (think "What do you like about math?" or "What do you want to accomplish in this class?"). If a performance orientation appears in those conversations, teachers can show the student how they'll have multiple opportunities to demonstrate what they know and ample time to learn the most essential skills. Teachers can outline the various ways students can progress through the content—different ways to practice, opportunities to apply learning, and so forth. With this pretext on the table, student and teacher can then work together to set a short-term goal that focuses on making progress toward their ambition using the tools most appealing to them.

Students can also come into a subject believing they're destined to fail, even saying "I'm not a writer" or "I never get math problems right." For these students, a goal-setting conversation can be an opportunity to reflect on previous learning experiences to understand the reasons behind that negative self-image. By learning more about how the student was asked to learn a subject in the past, their teacher can present different types of activities to set up their future learning. A goal for this type of student can focus on getting accustomed to a new way of thinking about a subject and finding learning strategies that grow their self-confidence and increase their ability to master new material.

What are the major takeaways from the research on academic culture, academic press, and autonomy support?

▶ First, supporting students with academic press is not a whole new way of teaching that requires teachers to throw out all their lesson plans and start over. Effective teaching still requires the combination of high-quality curriculum, age-appropriate instructional techniques, and balanced assessment. An academic culture that leads to student learning works because it is supported by these techniques, not replacing them.

▶ Second, a positive academic press can and should be part of schooling from the very beginning of a student's education. While motivating a 16-year-old can look a lot different from motivating a six-year-old, practices that encourage students to learn can drive success at any age. Teachers do not need to choose between supporting students emotionally and having high academic expectations. Goal setting is a key part of instructional practices that empower all students to learn.

▶ Finally, autonomy support provides an on-ramp for students to access a positive academic culture. Teachers can't control how goals are understood and used in the broader culture. What they can do, from the earliest ages, is provide students with opportunities to choose goals that reflect a focus on self-improvement and mastery. Because we all learn by doing, autonomy support ensures that a positive academic culture sticks by giving students the chance to practice.

 **REFLECT**

In this chapter, we'll focus on how to prepare a grade-level standard for goals, focused on ensuring that students at any achievement level can set goals that express a positive academic culture. To prepare for that process, select a standard that is part of the major work of your grade level; ideally, the standard should be one you have lots of experience with.

Consider the following questions, and jot some notes about your answers:

- What is the culture of the classroom like when this content is taught?

- What do students do while they're learning the content? How do those actions interrelate with what standards call for?

- What kinds of questions do they ask each other?

- How do they make connections between that content and what's going on in their daily lives?

- If those connections do not come easily for this standard, how can you support students in making personal connections to the content? How can you adjust or shift your planning processes to help students understand both standards and their shorter-term goals?

_____

_____

_____

GROWTH MINDSET AND RESILIENCE AS ONGOING

One of the prevailing concepts in social-emotional learning is the distinction between "fixed mindset" and "growth mindset." Popularized by the work of Dweck (2008) and others, growth mindset theory posits that students who believe intelligence can grow and change over time are more likely to grow than students who don't. In contrast, students with a fixed mindset believe that intelligence and ability are stable and related to unchanging personal factors, a self-fulfilling prophecy that prevents them from learning by inhibiting their motivation to try.

As an idea, growth mindset has exploded: You can find it referenced on countless classroom bulletin boards and spoken of in many school assemblies. Rare is the school where growth mindsets and fixed mindsets aren't an active part of the pedagogical conversation. Focusing on student mindsets makes a lot of sense, especially when aligned with setting mastery goals and motivating students to understand their own ability to learn.

But as with many educational fads before it, the devil of growth mindset is in the details. The evidence of the overall impact of growth mindset interventions is relatively weak and varies based on how the studied programs are designed (Sisk et al., 2018). Even Dweck has expressed reservations about the explosion of growth mindset adherents, fearing it has led to practices that focus on using "fixed mindset" as a label for students that justifies a lack of learning progress rather than using the growth mindset theory to point students toward a positive orientation. "The path to a growth mindset," Dweck (2015) writes, "is a journey, not a proclamation." Interventions that actually develop a growth mindset, in other words, focus on helping students become more growth-oriented over time rather than putting students' mindsets into one of two boxes.

 ## WHEN STUDIES SHOW NO IMPACT

Reading a study like the one by Sisk et al. (2018) that shows that growth mindset has little impact on student achievement can be discouraging. The study implies that certain kinds of instructional techniques—

(Continued)

(Continued)

including some that make real intuitive sense—don't work. As such studies pile up, they can easily lead teachers into a sense of defeat; it looks like nothing works to motivate student learning. But it's important to view these studies in the context of what they're trying to do.

The study by Sisk et al. (2018) is a meta-analysis, similar to the one by Hattie (2021) discussed in the introduction: It attempts to sum up the results of multiple studies to understand the overall impact of a common practice. Those studies took place in real classrooms with real teachers, who were likely all using different strategies to develop a growth mindset with their students. If the original studies are well designed, they've carefully isolated the specific and unique impact of a particular set of teaching materials, curriculum, teaching strategy, or the like. Meta-analyses rely on the kinds of measures that are easiest to gather together, such as standardized test scores. This means that it's very difficult for a wide-ranging study like Sisk's to be able to capture accurate data about qualitative skills, including growth mindset. For the most part, researchers can't isolate the effects of growth mindset as part of an overall strategy for students beyond the impact of a specific instructional program. Orienting students around a growth mindset is a practice that can involve many different instructional strategies and many different contexts, making it a difficult initiative to study as a whole.

Although studies designed like these are used by policymakers and researchers to make large-scale decisions about how to prioritize funding and attention, such studies are not designed to tell individual teachers how to work with individual students. For that, it is always important to combine an understanding of the research with other sources of information: the experience of colleagues, your personal educational philosophy, and the close knowledge you have of your students. A meta-analysis showing a low effect size does not necessarily mean that the practice does not work; it may simply indicate that the specific approaches teachers used in the gathered studies were not effective—or that their effects could not be measured.

TEACHING RESILIENCE

Focusing on the journey toward a growth mindset and an attitude of resilience is how Courtney, the first-grade teacher from the start of this chapter, introduces goal setting to her students. She starts, she told me, by tapping into the universal desire her students have to grow: "No one wants to stay the same." At the same time, she acknowledges the challenges of trying something new before you've had the chance to get good at it. "We teach the power of 'yet'—that's our magic word," Courtney says. Just because a student cannot yet do something doesn't mean their skills will stay at that level forever.

Closely tied to a focus on growth is building positive self-esteem through what Courtney labels *resilience*. Her students go through exercises to think about what receiving a compliment sounds like and feels like. They practice engaging in positive self-talk and having the courage to persist through a difficult challenge. Courtney also points out resilient characters during read-aloud activities and asks students to reflect on what that character did to overcome their initial difficulty. These lessons in resilience reinforce the idea that student skills are malleable and that students have the capability to grow and develop. Most importantly, Courtney's work teaches students that resilience is a practice, not an innate quality: All her students become more resilient over time.

By talking in general terms about how people get better at things, Courtney helps students understand that the purpose of goal setting is less about meeting a specific target and more about the learning that happens along the way. This includes nonacademic examples students are familiar with (learning to ride a bike, for example). It also includes introducing examples from her own life that allow students to see her empathy for the growth processes they're undertaking. "If I share times that I failed, or something didn't go my way, and what I did, that can go a long way," she notes.

She also highlights for students the opportunities they have to change their path to make their goal more accessible. "If it doesn't work out the first time, what's your tool belt of strategies to help you either adjust the goal or achieve the goal?" she asks. Students in Courtney's class identify their "helper people," the peers who can help them better understand a concept they're struggling with or motivate them to persist in trying to reach their goals.

Using Growth Mindset to Start a Conversation

By itself, the language of growth mindset may have a fairly limited impact on the educational success of students. Courtney uses this language in a different way—as an entry point to a conversation about what a student wants their goals to be. Rather than a one-time lesson, Courtney weaves thinking in growth mindset terms throughout her talk as a teacher and into multiple reflection opportunities for students.

In this framework, growth mindset fills an important function, reinforcing student self-esteem and making sure students enter into goal setting with the right intentions in mind. But growth mindset is not expected to do the heavy lifting of building a collaborative teacher-student relationship focused on learning.

How might this process apply to older students? By the time students enter middle and high school, they've been exposed to what researchers call *stereotype threat*, the pernicious set of social biases that say a specific gender, race, or ethnicity of students is better or worse in certain content areas. Research finds that these stereotypes produce some of the worst forms of fixed mindset (Spencer et al., 2016). For example, when female students perform worse on math than male students, the discrepancy may be attributable not to differences in ability but instead to the intense pressure the stereotype places on boys to succeed or the demotivation that comes from girls believing they can't achieve at a high level.

Many different types of interventions by teachers have been shown to diffuse stereotype threat by providing students with opportunities to reflect on their interests and strengths or witness the value of their hard work. A focus on growth mindset for older students could, for instance, apply Courtney's focus on building resilience and add age-appropriate opportunities for students to reflect on the origins of stereotype. These real-world conversations can set the stage for goal setting by building empathy between teachers and students, circumventing stereotype threat before it has a chance to impact student performance and provide students with the mental models they need to combat stereotype threat when it does emerge.

The jury is still out on whether growth mindset automatically produces improved achievement for students. What does seem clear is that merely making a growth mindset bulletin board or focusing on labeling students isn't enough to see change. Courtney's practice shows how growth mindset can introduce students to a way of thinking about their growth that can ensure that the goal-setting process is successful.

 **PLAN**

Recall the standard you reflected on in the REFLECT exercise of this chapter. Consider the ideas you jotted down about what a positive classroom culture looks like when students are learning about the standard. What do students need to be able to think and do in order to engage in those behaviors?

Think about what a behavioral or mindset goal that supports the academic standard might look like. How would you talk to students about their mindsets in advance of setting that goal—either in the whole group or one on one? How might you differentiate that goal for a student with a high level of existing resilience versus one with a low level of resilience? Write down two or three examples of resilience goals that can help your students meet the standard.

_____

_____

_____

ACADEMIC STANDARDS AS THE BASE FOR GOALS

Even for students in an appropriate state of mind, setting good goals requires consistent practice to get it right. The teachers featured in this book all report challenges in directing student attention in the right ways and toward the right ends. With academic goals particularly, students need the support of educators who can guide them through content, help them understand the best way to get from a short-term goal to a longer-term objective, and ensure that their work achieves the right balance between grade-level and off-grade-level content.

Guiding students does not mean dictating their goals to them. Setting goals, especially for younger students, requires a careful balance between giving students autonomy and providing the support for them to set attainable, practical goals related to academic content. Chapter 6 describes striking this balance in greater detail. Even with heavy influence from a teacher, the student can still sit in the driver's seat by choosing the reasons why they're motivated to learn. The essential role of the teacher, then, is to bring that *why* together with a realistic, relevant, and focused plan to achieve the *what* that goes with the *why*.

There are many different strategies to build that plan, each more or less appropriate given the characteristics of your students. Let's look at three of these strategies: setting class learning targets and rubrics, breaking down learning targets through student self-assessment, and identifying goals at different levels of difficulty.

SETTING CLASS LEARNING TARGETS AND RUBRICS

Alyssa Nestler, a second- and third-grade teacher, describes how guiding a class through setting a class-level goal related to an academic standard can set the stage for individual goals that are also standards-based. In this strategy, a class-level learning target keeps all students focused on necessary academic content, while individual student goals represent specific students' needed areas of growth, interest areas, and individual motivators. "I'm going to have a learning target for every single lesson so that the students understand that everything we do has a purpose, has an objective, is important, and has value," Alyssa asserts. "If I don't have a learning target, we probably shouldn't be doing it."

She begins her unit-planning process by taking an academic standard and rephrasing it in student-friendly language, paring it down to essential elements. Although Alyssa removes extra words, she consciously preserves the academic language in the standard, wanting to give students the opportunity to probe critical terms.

In the next stage, Alyssa presents the student-friendly version of the standard to the class and walks through the standard word by word. Students do the work of breaking down the academic language, providing examples of what it looks like to synthesize a text or compare and contrast a text's stylistic elements. Preserving the academic vocabulary helps Alyssa personalize the target for the students and encourages them to predict what success looks like.

The scrutinized standard then becomes a class learning target, which goes on the whiteboard alongside examples of success in meeting the target. With the class standard identified, Alyssa can then move into individual student goal-setting sessions in which students identify specific texts, areas of focus, or other elements that will support them specifically in achieving the learning target.

Alyssa warns that it takes time for students to learn to set goals that are both meaningful and achievable: Independent goal setting can be, in Alyssa's words, "a really heavy cognitive lift for a child in third grade." But she also preaches the value of practice in helping students take that challenge on. She frequently uses goal setting with longer-term projects, particularly writing assignments, to give students the time necessary to set a challenging goal and work toward meeting it.

In a longer-term project, Alyssa also uses assignment rubrics to track progress with students. Rubrics ground goals in what's realistic for students by showing them how far they need to go to fully meet the standard. If, for example, a student who currently doesn't use transition words in their writing wants to include three or four transition words in a paragraph (in line with the standard), the rubric encourages the student to start with one or two transition words and work toward the full standard. Rubrics show learning is "a process, and they'll improve in the process, getting better as time goes on," Alyssa says.

Having those waypoints in mind can help keep goals realistic while also focusing students on achieving the standard. Most importantly, no matter how extensively students have interacted with the rubric in forming their goals, Alyssa always ensures that the goals themselves are written in the students' own words.

Building a culture where students are comfortable and eager to set goals is a long-term process. Early frustrations that come from setting unrealistic goals can inadvertently reinforce fixed negative mindsets or lead students to participate in goal setting exclusively out of compliance. Helping students not get ahead of themselves reinforces the value of academic growth without asking students to take on an impossible task.

Introducing a process focused on identifying learning targets and providing examples of performance allows Alyssa to successfully implement goal setting even before students have the experience necessary to make all of the decisions related to their goals. "Whatever you want their goal to be, you've taught them the rubric, you've given examples, you've modeled a thought process for them, and you've written your goal for them," she explains. "You've just made that thinking process—evaluating what you want your goal to be and how you chose your goal—really visible for them."

Before implementing this approach, Alyssa's students set goals that weren't meaningful or didn't address appropriate learning targets. As a result, their goals weren't connected to their curriculum or assessments. By grounding individual goal setting in a class learning target, Alyssa is able to continue providing students with opportunities to choose their goals while also ensuring that their goals are a meaningful part of their learning.

BREAKING DOWN LEARNING TARGETS THROUGH STUDENT SELF-ASSESSMENT

While Alyssa's rubric process is born out of writing instruction, the process of modeling a progression of learning for students applies to any subject in which proficiency grows over time. While some standards may not lend themselves to a strict rubric, an informal learning progression crafted with student-friendly language can help students understand the waypoints they will reach on the road to proficiency. One way to create such a learning progression is to ask students to identify their own understanding relative to mastery.

Educator Cara Holt begins this process with kindergarten and first-grade students as Alyssa does: breaking a learning standard down for students, identifying key academic terminology, and ensuring that all students understand the standard. Once they understand the standard, students are asked to rate their own understanding of the material (Holt, 2020). The scale for doing so might look something like this:

1. I can't do this yet. I need to review.

2. I can do some of this, but I probably need help.

3. I can do this independently. I understand it.

4. I am an expert at this. I can teach others to do it.

Generally speaking, each student should set a goal to get from 1 to 2, from 2 to 3, and from 3 to 4. What that progress looks like for each student will undoubtedly vary based not only on their self-rating but also on the processes and tools that work best for them.

Further, teachers can use these ratings to create nearly limitless opportunities for students to practice and improve. Students at Levels 3 and 4 can help students at Levels 1 and 2. Each group can receive targeted support focused on raising them to the next level. Students in each group can work together on identifying and correcting misunderstandings.

Particularly for young students, self-rating can provide students with a measure of learning that's easy to understand and act on. Self-assessment can be useful as a benchmark for goals where students aren't ready to interpret assessment scores/letter grades or goals where those types of assessments don't make sense. Chapter 4 describes a variety of other formative assessment strategies that can provide tent poles around which students of all ages can set goals that are meaningful and accessible to them.

IDENTIFYING GOALS AT
DIFFERENT LEVELS OF DIFFICULTY

Another method of creating a trajectory of learning comes from Marzano's (2009) New Taxonomy. Marzano suggests four levels at which students can set goals. Because each of these levels can exist within the same content area of focus, they provide an opportunity to set unique goals for each student based on their current readiness. Providing appropriate challenge—not too much, not too little—is key to ensuring that students are engaged without being discouraged. Figure 2.1 shows how a standard can support learning at each of Marzano's levels.

Figure 2.1 Breaking Down a Standard Using Marzano's Taxonomy

Standard CCSS.ELA-Literacy.RI.5.3: Explain the relationships or interactions between two or more individuals, events, ideas, or concepts in a historical, scientific, or technical text based on specific information in the text.		
Level 1	Retrieval	I can correctly identify the different roles held by historical figures in this week's reading.
Level 2	Comprehension	I can describe how one event in this week's reading led to the events that came after it.
Level 3	Analysis	I can compare the relationship between the two historical figures in this week's reading with relationships between other figures I've read about before.
Level 4	Knowledge Utilization	I can apply the "lessons learned" in the scenario in this week's reading to resolve a modern-day problem or situation.

Level 1, **retrieval,** focuses on "the recognition and recall of basic information and the execution of procedures" (Marzano, 2009, p. 27). Goals at this level focus on how students produce something from memory or execute a series of steps. A Level 1 math goal might focus on computing a solution to a problem. In language arts, a Level 1 goal might involve identifying the features of a particular genre of literature or the form of an argument. Verbs that frequently appear in Level 1 goals include *recognize, select from, identify*, and *determine.*

At Level 2, **comprehension,** students focus on identifying and representing major ideas and supporting details. Goals at this level often require students to integrate, paraphrase, or summarize their

Level 1 knowledge. A math task could involve explaining how to measure area or represent percentages in graphical form. In language arts, students may be asked to summarize a story or identify key details of characterization.

Level 3, **analysis**, focuses on extending knowledge into "higher order" inferences such as categorizing, distinguishing between two ideas, or creating analogies and metaphors. Level 3 goals frequently go beyond what has been taught in class to new areas of understanding. Math tasks at Level 3 could involve analyzing your own problem solving for errors or identifying misunderstandings. In language arts, analysis goals may involve making an argument or predicting a character's future behavior outside the story.

At Level 4, **knowledge utilization**, students use their new knowledge by participating in a task related to real-world issues. The analysis present in Level 3 is applied at Level 4 to scenarios based in solving problems. In math, Level 4 goals ask students to select strategies for particular situations. In language arts, students may be asked to pick a strategy to understand an unfamiliar word or learn something new.

It's unlikely that every student will have the opportunity to set goals at each of these levels for all, or even most, of their essential standards in a given year. You may not have the time to address each level within whole-group or small-group instruction. What's key is not touching each level each time but taking advantage of the focus these learning levels provide on how students think about and act on their learning standards and goals. These levels can help students better understand what each standard entails and help them understand a pathway from beginning to advanced-level skills. Making goals specific and placing them at the right difficulty level makes it more likely they'll enhance student achievement (Marzano, 2009).

 **ACT**

Practice each of the strategies for using academic standards—setting class targets and rubrics, breaking down learning targets through self-assessment, and identifying goals at different levels of difficulty—to build a learning pathway around the standard you selected for the REFLECT and PLAN exercises in this chapter. First, consider how you will probe academic language with students and identify the key terms students can use to form their goals. Second, consider what goals you would suggest for a student at each of the four self-assessment levels. Finally, consider what goals could be suggested at each of Marzano's four levels of difficulty. Compare the goals created by these strategies. What goals are most appropriate for this particular standard, and why?

PRACTICE MAKES GOAL SETTING COMMONPLACE

By providing all these strategies, the intent isn't to overwhelm you but to show you that any standard can lend itself to student goals that are individual, rigorous, and attainable, regardless of grade level or individual readiness. Goals are a framework that students—all students—can use to understand their current learning and to make plans to move that learning forward.

The process of setting goals also provides a critical opportunity to engage students in relationships focused on learning. The teachers whose work appears in these pages emphasized the central importance of building quality relationships with their students—the most important prerequisite to learning. Goal setting bookended with content focused on academic press—the idea that every student can and will learn—helps students build the self-confidence, persistence, and shared ownership that drive an effective classroom.

Alyssa refers to this process as "freedom within form": giving students the amount of autonomy appropriate given their decision-making ability while also providing the guidance they need to ensure that their goals are focused on their best opportunities to learn. Freedom within form, or what researchers refer to as *autonomy support*, is the most sustainable route toward student ownership of learning, which helps students reach their potential and ensures that their interest in learning continues long after leaving the classroom.

None of these skills come to students or teachers without a lot of practice. While it's never too late to start goal setting, providing opportunities to set goals early in elementary school helps ensure that students make goals a part of their educational routines as they proceed

> *Freedom within form, or what researchers refer to as autonomy support, is the most sustainable route toward student ownership of learning, which helps students reach their potential and ensures that their interest in learning continues long after leaving the classroom.*

through the middle and upper grades. The form that goal setting takes—and the types of evidence teachers use to support goals along the way—are equally important. In the next chapter, we'll explore in depth the use of one-on-one conversations as the cornerstone of successful goal setting and how frequent formative assessment supports goals by giving students meaningful and accessible insight into their own learning.

CHAPTER SUMMARY

> Goal setting can happen in any type of classroom and in any grade, so long as it taps into the types of aspirations students express at that level.

> Taking students through the process of setting goals helps build a culture of academic press, one that encourages students to achieve high learning targets and provides ample support to help them get there.

> Using growth mindset can help students begin to think about their growth in positive ways and combat harmful stereotype threats.

> Beginning from academic standards, teachers can provide students several scaffolded opportunities to break learning targets into their own language and write short-term goals that work toward long-term mastery.

BUILD THE HABIT

One of the keys to writing good music, according to composer Adam Neely, is repetition. Repeating a key idea—no matter how unusual or "wrong" that idea may feel initially—makes the idea seem normal and common. "Repetition legitimizes" (Neely, 2019). While the verses of a song are important, it's the chorus that sticks in our minds and is the easiest way to identify the focus of the song.

Good learning habits can be conferred in much the same way: Students may not have lots of experience with the habit of goal setting or may think that goal setting isn't for them, but frequent practice can help make the habit routine. Engaging in the same positive habits over and over again will lead students to gradually build those habits into their identities as learners, see them as a natural extension of how they learn, and become better and better at maximizing the habits' potential.

Students evolve and grow as learners as the result of how they engage with learning. As described in the last chapter, academic press establishes a culture in which all students can and are expected to learn. The next step is to put in place regular activities that allow students to drive their learning, show students how their peers learn, and provide opportunities to celebrate success.

Goal setting is one of these activities. Engaging with goal setting is a great reminder for students—and teachers—that intelligence is malleable and that hard work is the most important factor in growing it. Still, embracing autonomous goal setting may not feel natural for students accustomed to more didactic forms of teaching. But repetition legitimizes. Providing students with many opportunities to set, revise, and reflect on goals offers them the chance to develop their goal-setting muscles, making it more and more a part of their learning routine.

This chapter focuses on the single most important habit of high-quality goal setting: the one-on-one conversation. Teachers who are developing highly effective goal setters conference with their students on a regular and ongoing basis to reflect on what makes for good goals, to set goals, to monitor progress on goals over time, and to understand results. These conversations help build student habits by ensuring the goals they set aren't a "one-and-done" exercise but instead are a central part of organizing what goes on in the classroom. They also help cultivate the relationships between students and teachers that lie at the center of high-quality learning.

LEARNING IS A FUNCTION OF HABITS

For much of the history of schooling, many people believed a student's intelligence was set in stone. The culmination of this argument was *The Bell Curve*, a 1994 book by psychologist Richard Herrnstein and political scientist Charles Murray that argued that intelligence measured by IQ scores is largely determined by birth and is unchanging across life (Herrnstein & Murray, 1994). They used this premise to support a number of troubling and racist conclusions: that IQ predicts a student's success in school and in life, that achievement gaps between white students and students of color are an inevitable outcome of biology, and that schools play a very small role in how students learn.

If this conception of how students learn were true, then goal setting wouldn't matter that much. Learning would move like a train: forward in only one direction, its speed determined largely by the power of the engine. The best-laid plans for student learning by teachers would be largely irrelevant to students' movement along that track.

Fortunately, we now know how false the ideas spread by *The Bell Curve* are. The book itself rests on fundamental flaws in both logic and statistical reasoning (Gould, 1994; Kardon, 1996). Rather than being solely a function of biology, learning is part of a complex and dynamic relationship between the brain and the contexts in which humans live their lives (Cantor et al., 2019). In that relationship, students are "active agents in their own learning" (p. 310): Their mindsets, motivations, and activities push learning toward or away from particular ends. Most importantly, students (like all of us) don't engage this process on their own: They are surrounded by a culture and set of conditions that change mindsets, provide motivations, and reward different activities.

Some students may appear to have decided exactly what kind of learner they are, what they are and aren't capable of. But young minds are malleable: Students have the opportunity to change their minds. The six-and-a-half hours students spend in class most days let their teachers provide them with rich opportunities to engage in the kinds of activities that lend themselves to developing a growth mindset, build positive relationships, and support learning. In trying to influence how students see themselves as learners, repetition legitimizes: It makes the kinds of learning behaviors that once seemed impossible instead feel normal.

 **REFLECT**

What are some regular learning habits in your classroom? How do these habits contribute to a learning culture, either positive or negative? What is your role in influencing those habits?

THE FOUNDATION OF A GOOD GOAL: A ONE-ON-ONE CONVERSATION

One-on-one conversations with students are the foundation of an effective goal-setting practice. As discussed in greater detail in Chapter 5, goals must be personal in order to be truly relevant for learners. While class-level goals can help guide instruction and provide students with ways to connect with one another, personal learning goals let students convert their dedication to the learning of their class into the self-confidence and agency necessary to see themselves as ambitious learners.

One-on-one conversations are invitations to students to engage in co-constructing their goals with their teacher. In one-on-one conversations, teacher and student work together to understand how the student is learning, what the student's next goal should be, and what the student should do in order to get to that goal. They leave the conversation having plotted or better understood together that student's learning journey, with each of a student's goals serving as another mile marker on the road.

These conversations also provide the teacher with the chance to do some intelligence gathering on student needs. While some students are eager to volunteer all the details about their lives, others need support to reveal everything the teacher needs to know to best serve them as an instructor, an advocate, or a mentor. One-on-one conversations provide the appropriate environment to ask probing questions about a student's strengths and the barriers to their learning that they can identify. I spoke with STEM teacher Matthew Marchoyok, who works with middle and secondary students on college and career readiness, and leverages goals as an important part of tying what he teaches directly to student concerns. "Conversation and connection," he says, "are applications of learning."

The types of questions you ask in a goal-setting conversation and the language used in those questions communicate to students how you understand learning and play a major role in how they come to understand learning. When crafting your language, focus on student strengths and opportunities for growth rather than the places they've fallen short. Where possible, create opportunities for students to make meaning of their learning rather than making that meaning for them. Use questions to elicit evidence of students' thinking rather than opportunities to introduce your own perspectives.

Instead of . . .	Try asking . . .
Why don't you like school?	How do you like to learn?
What are your weaknesses in math?	What do you want to learn next?
Why aren't you studying?	What helps you study at your best?
What grade do you want to get?	What do you want to know how to do?

To be most effective, those conversations and connections should be frequent—for example, held monthly or even weekly with each student. There's no doubt that such an investment of time is significant for any teacher, and the commitment may seem daunting at first glance. There are a few ways to make this challenge more manageable:

▶ Consider how existing structures in your classroom can support goal setting. Many classrooms use reading and writing workshops or math groups in which teacher/student conferring is already an important component. These conferences provide a natural opportunity to think about a student's goals, and a goal-setting process can be easily folded into these existing conversations.

▶ Keeping the conversations informal may make things easier. Oftentimes, short, frequent conversations can have more impact than longer, more scripted ones. While this chapter provides a series of tools to guide goal-setting conversations, some of these check ins can focus on updating an existing plan for a student rather than making a whole new plan.

▶ Track conversations in the way that makes the most sense for you. It's not necessary to keep an extended, formal report from each time you sit down with a student. Instead, something like an ongoing page in a notebook (or document on a computer) for each student can provide a quick way to jot down evidence of their progress toward a goal or considerations for your next conversation. Wherever possible, involve students in keeping their own logs of conversations with tools like those provided at the end of this chapter.

While the initial time investment in a goal-setting process can be substantial, goal setting in the long term can create greater efficiency in your planning by more equitably sharing responsibilities between teachers and students. When students can take greater control over their learning, they're able to become more self-directed, engage in more activities without direct teacher supervision, and make more choices about what they're ready to learn next.

ARTIFACTS, QUESTIONS, AND EVIDENCE OF LEARNING

There are three important resources teachers should bring to goal-focused conversations: artifacts, questions, and evidence.

Artifacts of learning are an important place to start goal-focused conversations. These artifacts can be completed projects, formative assessments, or any other learning product that can provide a jumping-off point for the conversation about where the student will go with their learning. Beginning with a student's work directs attention to how the student has demonstrated learning in the past and provides a seamless transition to talking about how they will do so next time. Using these artifacts helps conversations stay specific and focused rather than generally touching on a student's effort across a time period. Artifacts also give the student something to reflect on after the conversation concludes.

Bringing thoughtful **questions** to the conversation helps the teacher learn as much from the interaction as the student does. Instructional coach Erin Whitlock, who works with K–12 teachers throughout the state of Oregon, encourages teachers who are developing goal-setting practices in their students to focus on asking questions and putting the student in charge of making meaning out of their educational experiences. Students' answers serve as a critical source of information on what motivates them, what challenges they are experiencing in their learning, and how the teacher can better support their learning both inside and outside the classroom.

Asking younger students questions with more structure can provide them some autonomy without losing the benefits of student empowerment. First-grade teacher Courtney Pawol told me that starts her conversations by showing students an artifact and asking how well they think they performed on the task. She then asks them to decide "what we are going to do next." By building on the students' responses, she helps them make connections between their ideas and the academic strategies she has taught. In reading, Courtney frequently frames this conversation around the idea of "dropping a bad habit and picking up a good habit": substituting a less effective reading strategy (mumbling or giving up mid-word) for a more effective one (checking the picture or looking for context clues). Each of these strategies has a check box in her note-taking system, making it quick and easy to record which strategies the student has agreed to drop and which they've agreed to pick up. The simple act of letting the student choose from among these known effective strategies provides a much stronger sense of autonomy than trying to force the student into a strategy they didn't choose.

Finally, introducing **evidence** of students' learning progress on the path to their end goal can keep students grounded in reality and counteract negative mindsets. Some students, sixth-grade teacher Caryn Miller says, are their own harshest critics. The mindsets students bring into the classroom can lead them to view their learning purely in terms of success or failure. When this comes up, Caryn says, teachers should focus on redirecting students toward keeping their confidence high by presenting the student with documentation of their improvement over time. Emphasize that mistakes and errors are an inherent part of ambitious learning. As Erin puts it, "learning is what happens when we make mistakes."

💬 THE FEATURES OF A GOAL-SETTING CONVERSATION

Although goal-setting conversations don't all need to adhere to a rigid, formal structure, they should include the following elements:

1. **Checking in** on how the student is feeling about their learning, including their social-emotional well-being

2. **Clarifying** the student's learning target, helping them understand key ideas, and ensuring that they understand the importance of what they're about to learn

3. **Understanding** the student's current achievement through artifacts and evidence of learning (formative assessment information, discussed in greater detail in the next chapter, can be very useful here)

4. **Restating** the learning target as a specific, engaging, and appropriate goal

5. **Setting an action plan** for meeting the goal, including the steps the student will take, when the work will be done, where it will be done, whom the student can partner with to support their work, the materials they need to support their work, and how their learning will be measured

6. **Setting a timeline** for you and the student to follow up on how learning is progressing toward the goal, potentially involving families in the process

7. **Monitoring** student progress toward the goal as they complete it

8. **Assessing** student progress and celebrating success at the end of the goal period

There is no harm in keeping the boundaries around these features somewhat fluid. Each student will bring to each conversation a different understanding of formative evidence of learning, different levels of interest, and even different energy levels from day to day. The most important part of goal-focused conversations is to keep students engaged, demonstrating an ongoing interest in their learning and drawing them into a dialogue on the next steps in their learning.

STRUCTURING YOUR CONVERSATIONS

By now, it should be obvious that you and your students have a lot to talk about—likely more than can be included in a single conversation. It's not necessary for every goal-focused conversation to touch on every part of the goal-setting process. Chappuis and Stiggins (2020) identify six different types of conferences around goals:

1. **Feedback** conferences focus on reviewing learning artifacts and identifying next steps toward a learning target.

2. **Goal-setting** conferences focus on considering where the student is now and setting a new goal.

3. **Progress** conferences focus on examining where the student is relative to their goal.

4. **Achievement-status** conferences focus on sharing results from an assessment.

5. **Showcase** conferences focus on allowing the student to demonstrate their mastery of content.

6. **Intervention** conferences focus on an area of academic concern, allowing participants to make plans to remedy that concern.

This categorization isn't meant to be a checklist; teachers don't need to use every type of conference to tick off the box. Some may not be appropriate for certain students or at certain times in a progression of learning. Teachers may find themselves mixing and matching elements of different types of conferences to fit a particular situation. Instead, this breakdown provides a glimpse into the main ideas around which teachers can orient a goal-focused conversation and how interactions with students around their goals can shift over time.

While student and teacher are necessarily integral to one-on-one conversations about goal setting, it may be beneficial to expand the conversations to include a student's peers or caregivers as well. Involving caregivers and family in a showcase, achievement, or goal-setting conversation can be a great way to build a student's academic support network. Some teachers use these as a three-way parent-teacher conference model, where the student takes charge of showing their family what they've learned, what they're preparing to learn next, and how the family can support their learning progress.

Getting students accustomed to the regular rhythm of conversations can be a challenging task. As an introduction to the process, Erin recommends that teachers start with a conversation in which they engage the student in goal setting "before you name it." Prior to referencing what good goals look like, talk to students about something they want to accomplish, why they want to accomplish it, and what they need to do to accomplish it. This conversation need not be about academics; in all likelihood, it won't be. Instead, it is a model for the types of conversations the teacher and student will have in the future and lets the student quickly get accustomed to the goal-setting process. The conversation can also prompt important reflections on how the student engages with goal setting: Erin asks students how it felt to focus on a goal and prompts them to give her feedback on how she supported their progress toward their goal. In answering these questions, she says, students are both informing her about the next steps she should take and beginning to take ownership of the goal-setting process.

 **PLAN**

Take time to list some of the elements that you think should be included in your goal-focused conversations. What types of conversations do you anticipate having with students? For each of those types of conversations, what are some essential questions to ask students? How will you respond to their answers? How should the conversation end in order to stick in students' minds and set them up for effective learning?

TOOLS TO GUIDE STUDENT REFLECTION

Tools that guide reflection can help ensure that students bring the right information to goal-setting conversations and help connect those conversations with their progress. While it's important to avoid allowing a conversation to become solely about filling out the worksheet, the tools shown here offer ways that students can keep an ongoing record of their goals, be guided through identifying the elements of an appropriate goal, and record evidence of learning that can serve as a reference point throughout the year.

There is no best or worst tool among the seven shown here, nor do I recommend you copy one word-for-word out of this book to use in your classroom. These figures are examples of the forms a goal-setting tool can take, with the individual elements supporting student reflection and action. They are provided as sources of inspiration to help identify what will work best for your students, given their familiarity with goal setting, their age, and the types of goals that will best help them learn.

Figure 3.1 Early Elementary Example 1: Goals

Goal and strategies for (student name): _____

Goal:	Date:

Strategies:

What are my strengths?

What will I do if I get stuck?

Why is this goal meaningful for me?

Reflection/celebration

The "Goals" tool shown in Figure 3.1 focuses on reading and writing for early elementary students. The structure here is applicable for all types of goals, both academic and social-emotional. The substantial flexibility of this format allows younger students to create a kind of log of their one-on-one conversation and guides them to frame goals and strategies in their own words. Additionally, the focus on strategies in the Goals tool allows future conversations to focus on whether and how students used the strategies rather than a grade or other summative outcome.

Figure 3.2 Early Elementary Example 2: Goal Setting for Success: I Own My Learning!

Name: _____

My goal and why I'm setting it:		
How I'm learning (and why):	**Evidence of my progress:**	**Feedback:**
Date:		
Date:		
Date:		
Date:		
Date:		
Reflection and celebration:		

As students' goal-setting practice matures, they may be ready to be introduced to the idea of capturing learning through evidence. The tool labeled "Goal Setting for Success: I Own My Learning!" shown in Figure 3.2 extends the previous example by asking elementary students to record both their own evidence of their learning progress and feedback from their teacher. The use of an open-ended prompt—"How I'm learning (and why)"—lets students focus on the purpose behind each learning activity rather than the mechanics of the activity itself.

The Goal Setting for Success tool invites students to keep both sources of evidence in mind as they think about next steps in their learning. At the end of a goal, this tool also serves to support celebrating success by highlighting all the specific steps students took to reach their goal. Even if students do not meet their goal, this tool celebrates the effort put into their learning along the way.

Figure 3.3 Upper Elementary Example: My Learning Plan

Learning Objective: _____

For this learning objective, list your top two priorities. Answer the questions below for each on

01 I will work on:			
Can I do this by myself?			
☐ Yes	☐ No	If no, then who could help? ☐ Teacher ☐ Peer ☐ Family member	
		How likely am I to succeed? ☐ Not very ☐ Probably ☐ Likely	
My plan for action is:			

I'll monitor and celebrate my progress by:

02 I will work on:

Can I do this by myself?		
☐ Yes	☐ No	**If no, then who could help?** ☐ Teacher ☐ Peer ☐ Family member
		How likely am I to succeed? ☐ Not very ☐ Probably ☐ Likely

My plan for action is:

I'll monitor and celebrate my progress by:

With some goal-setting experience, students may be ready to consider the balance between ambitious and realistic goals. "My Learning Plan" shown in Figure 3.3 invites upper elementary students to choose their own learning priorities with open-ended language and also asks them to predict the likelihood of success along the way. Importantly, the tool doesn't discourage students from choosing more ambitious goals but instead prompts them to plan a system of support for achieving their ambitious outcomes. Used over time, this tool also allows teachers and students to reflect on the levels of challenge students gravitate toward and promotes reflection about students' goals to help them improve in the process.

Figure 3.4 Middle Grades Example: My Individual Goals

Name: _____ Date: _____

Area (check one):

☐ Reading   ☐ Work habits

☐ Math   ☐ Persistence

☐ _____

Target: _____

Where I'll focus and why:

_____

_____

_____

My plan of action:

_____

_____

_____

I will need the following help and resources:

_____

_____

_____

My timeline:

_____

_____

_____

As students gain both autonomy and experience with goal setting, they are ready to be given more responsibility. The "My Individual Goals" tool shown in Figure 3.4 maximizes student flexibility while still asking them to identify a specific goal, articulate a plan of action, and name the specific supports they will need to achieve that goal. This tool can be especially useful for middle grade students.

My Individual Goals is illustrated with both academic and social-emotional goals in mind, though it could easily be adapted to include others. Similarly, this example could be used with or without assessment scores in specific instructional areas as a target, depending on how an individual student is best motivated.

Figure 3.5 All Grades Example 1: Daily Learning Planner

Week of: _____ Name: _____

Monday

Learning goals and why:	How will I know I'm on the right track?
1.	1.
2.	2.
3.	3.
How did I do at meeting my goals?	What helped me the most today?

(Continued)

(Continued)

Tuesday

Learning goals and why:	How will I know I'm on the right track?
1.	1.
2.	2.
3.	3.
How did I do at meeting my goals?	What helped me the most today?

The tool shown in Figure 3.5, "Daily Learning Planner," is most suitable for students with a wide degree of autonomy and choice in the classroom—and it can be used with students in all grades. Particularly in upper grades, students may be charged with completing independent work under the general banner of a class set of learning targets and success criteria. This tool can be used with a whole class at the start of a lesson to record learning targets and success criteria, then could potentially function as an exit ticket for students to reflect on their learning when class is complete.

Figure 3.6 All Grades Example 2: My SMART Action Plan

Name: _____

My goal (SMART format: Specific, Measurable, Achievable, Relevant, Timebound):		

Strengths I can draw on and barriers to address so I can reach my goal:		

Action steps (include by when):	Progress check:	Revision (if needed):

Reflection and celebration:		

The most popular framework for understanding what makes an effective goal, for both children and adults, is the SMART goal framework. Borrowed from the world of organizational theory and business consulting and used in both academic and nonacademic contexts, SMART goals have the following characteristics:

▶ **Specific:** The goal leads the goal setter toward a concrete objective.

▶ **Measurable:** The goal setter has ways to determine whether (and the extent to which) the goal has been reached.

▶ **Achievable:** The goal can be realistically accomplished given the goal setter's timeline, current development, and so on.

▶ **Relevant:** The goal has meaning for the goal setter (not only for the teacher).

▶ **Timely:** The goal is designed to be accomplished within a specific period.

A variety of professional learning resources and books (Conzemius & Morganti-Fisher, 2012; O'Neill & Conzemius, 2006) discuss setting effective SMART goals. Students may already be familiar with setting SMART goals, which may make it easier to engage them in goal-setting practices. The tool in Figure 3.6, "My SMART Action Plan," may be more suitable for longer-term goals in which students identify specific action steps along a path toward a larger goal. This tool is also content agnostic, useful for both academic and social-emotional goals in all grades.

Figure 3.7 All Grades Example 3: Personalized Learning Plan

Learning goal:

Common Core State Standards addressed:
1.
2.

Evidence of learning	
At the end of this unit, I will be able to:	To demonstrate learning, I will:

My learning plan	
Why I will learn this:	What I need to know and understand:
I will accomplish this by:	How I'll know I'm on track:

Reflection and celebration of learning:

For students who are asked to focus their work around Common Core standards, the "Personalized Learning Plan" tool shown in Figure 3.7 makes connections between the standard and their goal more explicit. Particularly when breaking down standards as described in Chapter 2, this tool can guide students through understanding the relationship between a set of essential questions about a content area, the relevant standards, and the evidence they can use to demonstrate learning. After that group process, the tool could be used individually to help students in any grade model a specific goal that will help them answer the questions.

 **ACT**

Build your own goal-setting tool incorporating various elements from the exemplars, the list of important conversational elements you created earlier, and your own ideas. Consider how your tool will support conversations relating to goals at each stage: when a goal is developed, as you monitor progress toward the goal, and when you collaborate with your students to understand what they achieved.

REPETITION LEADS TO MEANING

Students at every stage of schooling are still in the process of building their identities as learners. For most of us, our experiences in school set perceptions of our own strengths and weaknesses that have stuck with us throughout our lives. Anyone who says they're "not good at math" or "not much of a reader" is probably thinking of an experience they had in school. These perceptions can shift, however, with the help of a quality educator. In each of the stories we tell about how we know we're good or bad at something, an educator likely had the opportunity to help us take a different tack or solve a problem in a different way.

In trying to build the right kind of culture in your classroom—one with both academic press and growth mindset—repetition legitimizes. What students do every month, every week, or even every day has a big impact on how they perceive themselves as learners and what they will ultimately achieve. Goals can provide a cadence to those months and weeks by giving regular, ongoing, and relevant touchpoints where teachers and students interact regarding student learning.

In repetition, human beings find patterns. In patterns, they find meaning. The meaning of learning is conveyed when, as an educator, you find opportunities to routinely influence how a student feels about themselves as a learner. One-on-one goal-focused conversations provide these opportunities as you orient a student's feelings toward success. The next chapter highlights how teachers can showcase success related to students' goals using both formative evidence of learning and advocating for students to reach for their personal best.

CHAPTER SUMMARY

▶ Repetition legitimizes: Continually practicing goal setting, no matter how unusual it appears to students at first, helps them build the positive learning habits that are essential for goal setting practices to succeed.

▶ Research has repeatedly shown that students' ability to learn is a function of their environment, supports, and habits rather than their background or personal characteristics.

▶ Frequent one-on-one conversations between students and their teachers improve student-teacher relationships, build the habit of goal setting, and provide a time and place for students to reflect on their learning progress and celebrate success.

SHOWCASE SUCCESS THROUGH BALANCED ASSESSMENT

Though the name may not suggest it, goal setting continues long after a student has set their first goal. In order to make goals successful, students need consistent opportunities to revisit their goal, monitor progress, and understand opportunities for further growth. They also need the positive reinforcement that comes from seeing their effort pay off: the opportunity to celebrate success. Those opportunities all come from assessment.

Assessment has a bad rap in American education, primarily because of some of the ways in which standardized tests have been used to characterize the work of teachers, administrators, and schools. For individual students, however, a balanced assessment system used appropriately provides the evidence and feedback that motivates those students to complete their goals and set future, more ambitious ones. Using assessments as part of goal setting, in other words, means nothing more (and nothing less) than bringing the right types of evidence to bear in order to demonstrate to students that goal setting is worthwhile.

Setting a successful goal requires giving students the chance to see their learning, to visualize success. Though students learn in a variety of ways, demonstrating that learning requires clear and uniform processes that they understand and that promote metacognition: intuitions by the student about how they are thinking.

Understanding assessment as a tool in the way this chapter describes it means treating each assessment as an opportunity to gather information about what students have learned. That information is incredibly useful when planning instruction that is focused on individual students' strengths and needs. Having and understanding that information is the fundamental right of every student as a learner.

A system with too little assessment asks students to run in place—to work as hard as they can but with no sense of moving forward.

It's unfair to ask students to invest time and energy into learning content without feedback on doing that successfully. It's inequitable for some students to receive less of that feedback or be more dependent on subjective interpretations of their performance. While a system with too much or the wrong balance of assessments distracts and takes time from learning, a system with too little assessment asks students to run in place—to work as hard as they can but with no sense of moving forward.

This chapter underscores how to use the three types of assessments in a balanced assessment system—formative, benchmark, and summative—to support and reinforce goals. Primary among these is formative assessment. Formative assessments and formative instructional practices, when done well, provide transparent evidence of learning, expose student misconceptions, and reinforce and build a vision of learning based on continuous growth and student ownership. Standardized benchmark and summative assessments provide a wider view of learning and motivate in different ways. When used appropriately, and with help for students to understand how these assessments work, these assessments can also contribute to goals that are focused on continuous growth.

SUPPORTING GOALS WITH FORMATIVE EVIDENCE OF LEARNING

A balanced and understandable assessment strategy begins with formative assessment: the many opportunities throughout instruction that students have to demonstrate learning and their teachers have to understand what students know and can do. When well-planned, frequent, and collaborative between students and teachers, formative assessment can both strengthen student learning and support the work of students owning their own learning (Formative Assessment for Students and Teachers State Collaborative on Assessment and Student Standards [FAST SCASS], 2018). Research has found consistent positive impacts on student achievement and growth from well-implemented formative assessment practices (Hattie, 2013; Kingston & Nash, 2011).

Figure 4.1 Formative Assessment Cycle

Where is the learner GOING?

CLARIFY LEARNING

Engage learners to understand what they're learning, why they're learning, and what constitutes success

ACTIVATE LEARNING

Empower learners to be instructional resources for themselves and others

Where is the learner NOW?

ELICIT + ANALYZE EVIDENCE

Employ multiple methods to gather evidence of each learner's thinking to inform next steps in the learning

PROVIDE ACTIONABLE FEEDBACK

Use learning-focused feedback to move learners forward

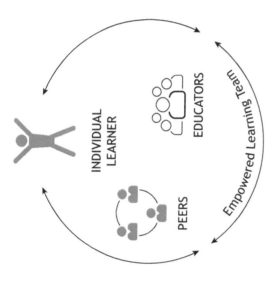

INDIVIDUAL LEARNER

EDUCATORS

PEERS

Empowered Learning Team

WHAT'S NEXT in the learning journey?

Effective formative assessment happens in a four-part cycle, as shown in Figure 4.1:

▶ First, teachers **clarify learning** by engaging learners in understanding what they're learning, why they're learning it, and what constitutes success.

▶ Second, teachers **elicit and analyze evidence**, employing multiple methods to gather evidence of each learner's thinking to inform next steps in the learning.

▶ Next, teachers **provide actionable feedback** by using learning-focused feedback to move learners forward.

▶ Finally, teachers **activate learners** by empowering learners to be instructional resources for themselves and others.

As they work through this cycle, learners, teachers, and peers collaborate around a process that drives learning forward through its focus both on supporting students and improving their understanding of what they've learned.

Student goal setting is merely another version of the formative assessment cycle. By working together, students and teachers examine learning targets to build a goal (clarifying learning). On an ongoing basis, they examine evidence of how a student is progressing in that learning (eliciting and analyzing evidence) and make adjustments to goals based on what that evidence finds (providing actionable feedback). Finally, they celebrate success to reinforce a positive learning attitude for students and their peers (activating learners). Each of the stages of the formative assessment cycle can be supported through and within the context of the one-on-one conversations highlighted in Chapter 3.

Understanding what formative assessment is and why it works provides an additional data-rich perspective on bringing goal setting into action. The steps above all require evidence of what a student has learned. As their teacher, it is up to you to provide opportunities for students to authentically and accurately demonstrate what they know. By using formative assessment intentionally and liberally, you can create those opportunities in the course of regular class work and a clear alignment between a student's goals, their measures of progress, and your daily instruction. This alignment makes it clear to everyone that goals are not a random exercise but are part and parcel of learning.

USING FORMATIVE ASSESSMENT
TO MONITOR STUDENT PROGRESS

The first and primary goal of formative assessment is accurately and authentically measuring student progress toward mastery. In meeting this need, formative assessments work together with all types of assessment. However, while standardized assessments can measure a student's general knowledge in a domain, they're not detailed enough to provide specific feedback about a particular academic standard or skill. This specific and precise information is invaluable in creating short-term goals focused on weekly growth.

When helping students master a standard, understanding and identifying their misconceptions is key. Say a student who is working on the coordinate plane in math plots a point in the wrong place. There are several reasons the student may have gotten that problem wrong: maybe they mis-numbered the quadrants of the plane, confused the X and Y axes, or even misunderstood the words *vertical* and *horizontal*. The simple act of providing students time to practice skills and observing how they practice those skills provides information that can illustrate their next steps and also demonstrates progress toward meeting a goal.

Many teachers formalize these types of observations using "probes": formative assessment strategies designed specifically to understand a student's current progress toward their goal (Safer & Fleischman, 2005). Short written or oral assessment activities conducted on a weekly, biweekly, or monthly basis can provide comparable information on how a student is doing relative to their mastery goals. When a student's rate of growth slows down, teachers can adjust instruction to support the students who need it the most. Students can also participate in this data-gathering process by graphing their data and building goals based on their own rate of growth.

Formative assessments also provide essential opportunities to demonstrate higher-level skills. In Marzano's (2009) New Taxonomy for breaking down standards, described in detail in Chapter 2, higher-level skills like analysis and knowledge utilization are difficult to explore in multiple choice assessments. Formative assessment provides tools for evaluating students' use of language: Teachers can ask students, for example, to write reflections on their learning, explain a concept to their peers, or divide into groups to debate an important issue. Much of ambitious instruction takes place in dialogue between students and teachers as teachers both elicit students' thinking and teach students how to use academic language (Heritage & Wylie, 2020). These types of conversations during instruction—when teachers prompt students to think in different ways, ask them to justify answers and build off their peers, and cultivate discussion and argumentation skills—are both a form of learning in themselves and a rich opportunity for teachers to gauge students' understanding.

It's for these reasons that formative assessment is sometimes called "assessment for learning" (Stiggins, 2002)—it integrates gathering evidence of student learning, giving feedback to students, and instruction itself into a seamless and consistent process (Cauley & McMillan, 2010). Goals bring to formative assessment ways of interacting with students around that learning: understanding new learning targets, analyzing evidence of that learning, and making plans for next steps. While this approach is effective for increasing student achievement and growth, it also has important ramifications for student engagement with learning.

USING FORMATIVE ASSESSMENT TO MOTIVATE AND EMPOWER

The same elements of student empowerment and insight that make formative assessment an effective intervention for achievement also give formative practices the ability to motivate and empower learners. Formative assessment stimulates metacognition: the process of thinking about thinking (Andrade & Brookhart, 2020). By asking students to reflect on a teacher's assessment of learning, participate in the assessment of peers, or even self-assess their own learning, we are also asking them to take greater control over their educational destiny.

When that control is cultivated, formative practices can promote stronger degrees of self-regulated learning (Makkonen & Jaquet, 2020). This means that students are more likely to keep track of their own progress, ask questions to improve their understanding, and identify different ways of improving their work. Research has found that these types of skills, combined with relevant useful feedback from a teacher, increase students' focus, keep lower-achieving students from avoiding work, and increase students' desire to master content (Andrade & Brookhart, 2020).

Formative assessments can also help align a goal with the mastery orientations that are critical for goals to succeed. Assessments can be an academic motivator and a useful target for goals if they are grounded in what the student already cares about (Usher & Kober, 2012). Motivating assessments are those that reward effort, encapsulate short-term goals, and give students notice of what will be assessed ahead of time, all of which are more possible with a formative assessment.

Further, while the content of standardized tests cannot be adapted to meet a student's interests or strengths, formative assessments can focus on areas that individual students find motivating and provide a basis for measuring success in an area that might otherwise be difficult to set a goal around. A student who wants to become a journalist, for example, is unlikely to see the relevance in an item bank from a standardized test. However, a teacher who asks the student to write a news story can use that activity to both check for mastery on key standards in writing and informational text and provide the student with a motivation based directly in their interests.

BRINGING FORMATIVE ASSESSMENT AND STUDENT GOALS TOGETHER

One of the key focus areas in middle school science is understanding the relationship between the earth and other bodies in the solar system. The Next Generation Science Standards ask students to observe, describe, predict, and explain the motion of the sun, the earth, the moon, and the stars together and understand how they relate to the intensity of sunlight on a given point on the earth, the seasons, and the position of each of those bodies (NGSS Lead States, 2013). A unit like this requires teachers to closely understand what students know, including the common misconceptions that come from not understanding how parts of the system work together. Because students are working with abstract concepts removed from their day-to-day lives, it can also present real challenges in helping them stay motivated.

Traditionally, a unit like this might be assessed through a summative test at the end of the unit. Students would be asked to review key vocabulary from the relevant textbook chapter—*revolution, axis*, and *orbit*—and to define these terms on the test. Once that test was graded, their teacher would have a reasonable idea of how well students understand those key terms. But a single multiple-choice test offers few opportunities for that teacher to understand how students think about planetary bodies as a system and no opportunity to confront student misconceptions as students are learning. More importantly, getting a good grade on that unit test is about the only form of motivation students have to succeed. As Chapter 1 showed, performance-based motivators have at best a weak impact on students and at worst perpetuate harmful attitudes about learning with unintended consequences.

Now imagine a version of this unit centered around frequent formative assessment and a class project: building a moving model of the solar system. At each step in the building process, the teacher has an opportunity to see in real time how students think about the movement of the planetary bodies. Students can also see each other's thinking, discuss differences of opinion, and use evidence to support their own positions. Students can set individual goals based on how they'll support the project: Maybe some students will work on the earth's rotation mechanism while others focus on modeling how the sun's position creates seasons and others work as fact checkers to double-check the details. The teacher can even check student knowledge of those vocabulary words but in an environment where mistakes are welcomed, students are encouraged to cooperate to come up with solutions, and the relevance of the learning is represented by a set of real-life objects sitting on the table in front of them.

The second version of this learning is a fundamentally different approach. In the second version, students are given power over their learning: They decide how to contribute to the project, how to represent the key ideas they're receiving in direct instruction, and how to resolve differences when their classmates come away with a different view. Tying this power to assessment—perhaps the most potent source of power in our educational system—ensures that this kind of learning will be seen as meaningful. While there are many ways to empower students by setting and meeting goals, building at least some of those goals around formative assessments communicates to students that demonstrating their learning is important and part of how you understand their success.

 REFLECT

Think about a lesson you taught recently that included elements of formative assessment. Consider how a student might plan a goal, starting from data gathered in that assessment. What will it show them about what they've learned already? How can you communicate the results of that assessment to make it clearer to them? How can you connect a learning target achieved at this developmental level with long-term goals and aspirations? What opportunities will they have in the coming weeks to revisit that assessment and discover what they've learned?

USING STANDARDIZED ASSESSMENT DATA AS PART OF GOALS

Formative assessments are particularly suitable to goal setting because of how frequently they're collected, the opportunity they provide students to practice and improve, and the relatively low-stakes environment in which they are often delivered. Formative assessments are by design a natural fit with a mastery orientation and so lend themselves readily to appropriate and motivating goals.

Many teachers also use standardized assessment data as part of student goals. Benchmark or interim assessments may, for example, help students project to a future score on a college entry exam or provide a bird's eye view of a student's growth and achievement over time that facilitates conversations about helping them get back to grade level. Whether for better or worse, these types of goals often have the most initial relevance for students, as they open doors to colleges and career pathways.

Ryan McDermott, who teaches seventh- and eighth-grade math, spoke to me about how he uses benchmark assessment data to help students probe skills they're missing prior to high school. Because student skills in mathematics tend to vary widely in these grades, Ryan came to goal setting as an effective method of setting learning paths based on where individual students came into the class. For Ryan, individualized instruction "all starts with the data, and it all starts with creating goals based on that data." Once students have completed their benchmark math assessment in the fall, he uses that data to structure their first one-on-one conference. In these conferences, he and the student will analyze data from the interim assessment, co-construct a learning target, and build goals around that target to work toward a different score on the next benchmark assessment.

For students, the value of using benchmark assessments as part of goal setting is in the ability to quickly identify what content and skills they are ready to set goals around next. Once that broad area of focus is found, it's easier to plan a set of targeted learning (including specific formative assessment activities) to help students progress toward mastery in specific skill areas. Particularly for middle grade teachers with a lot of students, this early and comprehensive look at their academic skills can help both students and teachers save a great deal of time in finding goals that are right for them.

For other students, setting a target based on benchmark or summative assessment data can be an anxiety-producing and defeating experience, linking their abilities as a learner to their performance in a single test event. Setting a goal may heighten the stakes of an assessment event for a student and turn them off from goals they feel they can't achieve without being "a good test taker." Integrating standardized assessment data may also lead to a reductionist approach in which students no longer consider other outcomes of their learning as meaningful or relevant.

Whether or not to use standardized assessment data as part of your goal-setting practice is a complicated question, and there are no easy answers. Just as standardized assessment data can be misused to put students in competition with one another or heighten anxiety around performance, activities that appear to be formative in nature can provoke many of the same emotions. Which assessments are appropriate for use in a goal, in other words, are less about the assessment itself and more about how it is used and its appropriateness for the individual student.

Chapter 1 identified the features of effective goals: They are individualized, focused on mastery, and both meaningful and attainable. These keys are particularly important to keep in mind when using standardized assessment data, which can paint students with a broad brush unless the data are put in the proper context. Before using standardized assessment data as part of a goal, it's worth taking time to become familiar with all the tools and reports an assessment offers to ensure that the goals you direct students toward are realistic for them.

FINDING WHAT'S ATTAINABLE

Assessments of all kinds—formative, benchmark, and summative—provide contextual information that can help encourage students to set goals that are both meaningful and realistic. Assessments can also help when discerning the right balance between what is meaningful and what is attainable for a particular student.

Assessments offer two main types of reference points for student performance: norm-referenced and criterion-referenced (American Educational Research Association, American Psychological Association, & National Council on Measurement in Education, 2014):

▶ Norm-referenced data compare students to their peers: They can show how one fifth-grader performed relative to all fifth-graders who took the test, all fifth-graders from a similar district, or fifth-graders with similar characteristics. In standardized benchmark and summative tests, this kind of data appears in the form of percentiles or research that correlates scores on one assessment to other measures of student performance. In formative assessment, you can think of other students in a class or school as an informal type of norm reference, demonstrating how students tend to progress through a particular set of academic standards.

▶ Criterion-referenced data show student scores as a measure of their knowledge and skills. They may, for example, show where a student is relative to a state standard for grade-level mastery or identify standards or skills the student is likely to know based on their performance on the assessment. Most assessments, and all formative assessments, have criterion-referenced data: They show what a student knows about a particular content area or construct.

Many standardized tests offer both norm-referenced information and criterion-referenced information, meaning the same assessment results can be understood in different ways.

In order to be both mastery-oriented and meaningful to students, goals should rely on criterion-referenced data. In order to set an effective goal, the student should know what areas of content they have already mastered and what standard or skill they should aim for next. Formative assessment plays an invaluable role by providing benchmarks to help students know whether or not they have met their goal.

Although goal setting should focus primarily on content, keep norm-referenced data in mind. Normative assessment data can describe how much growth in achievement students typically experience at a given achievement level and the extent of the supports needed to achieve above-average growth. Perhaps not surprisingly, these predictions bear out most of the time: Students are more likely to achieve goals that are close to the typical growth predicted by assessments (White et al., 1997).

When considering both types of assessment data, remember that no individual student's performance is ever set in stone; even growth at the 80th percentile is achieved by one out of every five students. When deciding which students should set goals for exceptional growth, consider the amount of time it would take for those students to catch up to grade-level standards, their past patterns of growth, and the types of supports you can provide to increase their likelihood of success. No assessment data can tell you exactly how far-reaching a goal should be, only how much encouragement and what resources are required to help get the student to that goal.

PLAN

First, write down a list of all the standardized assessments your students take during the year and when they take them. Next, write down some of the pros and cons of using standardized assessment information to set student goals. Looking at both lists, what are one or two standardized assessments that might lend themselves to effective goals? Identify these and consider when those goals could be set and what types of short-term activities would allow for goals in between testing events.

SETTING PERSONAL BEST GOALS

Beyond norm- and criteria-referenced assessment scores, one of the best points of reference to use for setting goals is students themselves. Personal best (PB) goal setting focuses on continuously working to better a previous best past personal effort, usually by reaching closer to mastery (Burns et al., 2018). Asking students to work toward a personal best is a simple and straightforward way to help manage some of the potential anxieties produced by assessment data and replace those anxieties with a clear mastery orientation.

PB goal setting builds on a research base that is separate but complimentary to the work on goals we've looked at to this point. Though derived separately, PB goals share many of the same characteristics as the traditional goal-setting practices considered here: They help direct attention and effort toward a target, give specific information on what a student needs to reach a goal, energize students to meet a goal, and look to increase student effort and autonomy (Martin, 2013). Where PB goals differ is in their focus on the numbers: asking students to either put more time and effort into *processes* (practice or studying) or into *outcomes* (performance on a test).

As a guide to learning, your understanding of what is attainable can help students more sustainably work to achieve their ultimate goal. If, for example, a student has gotten *D*s on their last three unit tests, asking them to get an *A* on the next test is probably unrealistic, even though it is an appropriate longer-term aspiration. Similarly, if that student has been studying 10 minutes a day, asking them to study for 30 minutes a day is likely to overwhelm and discourage them. Focusing on frequent incremental growth (a *C* on the next test, 15 minutes of studying a day) provides the building blocks of persistence that will be necessary for that student to reach their ultimate goal. In these areas, where research-based norms can't tell you what kinds of progress are typical for similar students, asking students to set a PB can ensure that goals are both attainable and ambitious.

THE RESEARCH ON PERSONAL BEST GOALS

PB goals tap into a student's ability to visualize the future they want for themselves and use that as a motivator for behavior (Burns et al., 2018). Research finds that PB goals have impacts on academic motivation and engagement even a year after the goal is complete (Martin & Elliot, 2016). For some students, these impacts may exceed the value of setting mastery-oriented goals without a target score (Collie et al., 2016). This may be because of additional social-emotional boosters to learning activated by PB goals (Liem et al., 2012). These include deep learning (complex engagement with academic content), academic flow (the subjective experience of being fully absorbed in a task), and academic buoyancy (the ability to bounce back after a typical academic setback).

The key mechanism that PB goals use to influence student motivation is self-competition. At least for some students, a strong sense of self-competition positively predicts engagement, achievement, and growth mindset (Burns et al., 2018). Similar to goals that are made applicable to a student's aspirations, self-competition is one motivator for students to create and complete goals that relate to students' interests and situations. Chapter 5 discusses creating relevant goals with students as a source of motivation in greater detail.

As described above, allowing PB goals to reinforce a positive sense of self-efficacy requires that those goals are both ambitious and realistic. While occasionally missing a goal target can be a formative experience in itself, regularly failing to achieve a goal promotes discouragement and ultimately disengagement. As translators of data, it's up to teachers to gently guide students toward PB goals that are comparable to how they've grown in the past and within reach over the timespan for which the goal is set.

> It's up to teachers to gently guide students toward personal best goals that are comparable to how they've grown in the past and within reach over the timespan for which the goal is set.

Goal theory has generally found that different goals bring with them different mental frameworks that tap into different sources of motivation (DeShon & Gillespie, 2005). While some goal orientations are counterproductive to learning and require careful redirection by teachers, PB goals do not necessarily work to mastery's detriment. Provided that assessments are well-designed, doing well on an assessment should also represent mastery, aligning PB goals with other learning priorities (Usher & Kober, 2012). The trick is ensuring that the assessments students use directly relate to classroom learning goals and that PB goals are promoted among the students who will best respond to them.

WHO DO PERSONAL BEST GOALS WORK WELL FOR?

Like all goal-setting techniques, PB goals will likely work well for some students and may work poorly for others. Some students may be more motivated by numerical accomplishments than others. PB goals may work better for students who are significantly under or over grade level, for whom the class's mastery targets may be less relevant or attainable. Martin (2013) documents specific success using PB goals with students with attention deficit hyperactivity disorder (ADHD), for whom PB goals may have particular benefits around self-regulation and executive function. For other students, focus on specific numerical targets might be a source of additional anxiety or may sour the relationship between student and teacher (Martin & Elliot, 2016). For these students, the focus in the next chapter on building relevance for goals is especially key.

Mastery and PB goals are complimentary approaches. While reaching for the same kinds of targets, mastery goals are framed in terms of learning and the task, while PB goals are focused on the self (Martin & Elliot, 2016). Ultimately, what a student aspires to accomplish with a PB goal should be pointed toward greater mastery of academic content, even if that specific mastery target isn't the center of the written goal. It may be that different academic content lends itself to either approach; if, for example, a specific mastery target is more obtuse or difficult for students to relate to, working on achieving a PB goal might be a more straightforward goal to set. It may even make sense to alternate between PB and mastery goals for individual students to allow them to experience both kinds of motivations and understand which works best for them.

As with all goals, the success of PB goals is highly dependent on the relationship between teacher and student (Collie et al., 2016). Students have to find their goals meaningful and must also trust that the assessments against which they are planning those goals are meaningful and fair. Constructed under the right conditions, PB goals can motivate extraordinary student effort. Whether that effort is directed toward learning depends on whether the assessments students are working to get better at are aligned with essential learning targets.

ACT

Design a conversation protocol for a goal-setting conference focused on establishing a personal best goal with a student. Consider first how you'll present assessment data. What is the right assessment to use? What reports or other methods of showing the data are available to you? How can you identify the level of growth that's meaningful and reasonable for an individual student? Next, think about who personal best goals might be right for. How will you identify those students? Finally, consider the key messages you'll give to students as they set a personal best goal. What can you say and do that will help students keep their focus on growth directed toward academic mastery?

FROM TESTING TO INVESTIGATING

By bringing assessment information into student goal setting, teachers reflect to students how a core classroom activity (assessment) relates to them. It also has the potential to contribute to the mindsets that lead students to metacognition. Throughout their schooling, we encourage students to be investigators: to use the scientific method, critical thinking skills, and reasoning to understand more about what they don't know and find solutions to emerging problems. Bringing the same ideas to bear on their learning requires that they have access to a body of evidence about that learning that they can understand and use to better understand themselves.

This chapter reflects how goals can help make assessments more relevant for students. In order for that to happen, however, goals themselves must align with students' ambitions, interests, and personal needs. The next chapter explores how to help students set goals that are relevant both to their individual interests and to the universal desire to grow and develop as a person. Along with providing ample amounts of student choice, relevance works to ensure that the content of goals motivates and inspires learning.

CHAPTER SUMMARY

> A balanced assessment system including formative, benchmark, and summative assessments provides the evidence of learning students need to act on their goals.

> Formative assessment practices provide in-the-moment evidence of student learning that can contribute to short-term goals, reinforce student ownership of learning, and be made easy for students to understand and act upon.

> Standardized benchmark and summative assessments can provide high-level information on student learning that is useful for setting goals that are ambitious and realistic.

> The personal best goals model is a method for keeping students' focus on content mastery and individual improvement even as they reflect on assessment data.

5

CREATE PERSONAL RELEVANCE

By the time they enter the classroom, your students have aspirations that mastering content can enable. Maybe they're working toward reading connected text or advancing their reading level to take on a popular novel. Perhaps they want to try their hands at programming a video game and need additional math skills to get them there. For many students, college may already be on their minds, and the need to get the right score on a college entrance exam looks like an insurmountable barrier.

For all their benefits, academic standards do not by themselves encapsulate the reasons why we learn. For one thing, our purposes for learning are rarely fixed: Students (and many adults) change how they understand their own purpose in the world on a regular basis. Every day brings a new set of ideas about what they can do and who they can be. Students don't just change their minds about who they want to be when they grow up; they change the books they want to read, the places they want to go, and the things they care about. All these motivations, even as they change, are ones teachers can tap into to make short-term goals more meaningful.

Connecting the purposes of students' learning with the purposes of their being—at least as they understand them right now—is a key part of the role of an effective educator. "Responsibility for learning," instructional coach Erin Whitlock told me, "comes in connecting the *do* of the learning to the *why* of the learning"—unlocking the purpose of learning something and helping students understand why that purpose matters.

Learning doesn't come with a built-in set of salespeople. It can be difficult for anyone, especially young students, to make the connection between their dreams and the classroom's focus on a particular day.

> While almost all students recognize that learning is important, some are simply not motivated by academics or love of learning alone. But maybe if that learning were reframed as a means to achieve a certain goal, these students would be better able to see its value. (Usher & Kober, 2012, p. 1)

Goal setting is your opportunity to sell the importance of learning by connecting it with sources of meaning in students' lives.

 ## KNOW, WONDER, VALUE, LEARN

Most teachers have interacted with the "Know, Want to Know, Learn" (KWL) model at some point in their educational careers (Ogle, 1986). This model calls on students approaching new content to first reflect on their prior knowledge (what they *know*) and their questions within that focus area (what they *want to know*). After a lesson is completed, students return to the activity to describe what they have *learned*. Several models of a 21st-century KWL approach now exist that asks students for other details that demonstrate their ability to reflect on learning.

Sixth-grade teacher Lindsay Deacon's version of this model includes an added space for students to record what they're interested in and what they value about a topic. By capturing this information early in a unit, Lindsay gets a quick look at the types of values she can tap into during a goal-setting conversation to amplify the student's interest in the learning topic. This kind of quick strategy helps immediately supplement what Lindsay knows about her students and activates their own thinking around how a set of learning may be relevant to them.

THE RESEARCH ON STUDENT MOTIVATION

What we as individuals find relevant derives from the ideas and emotions that motivate us and drive us toward action. Motivations shape the reasons that goals exist and in turn set the tone for the strategies students use to achieve those goals. While standards documents and curricular plans specify in detail what students should learn, they cannot dictate how students will feel about what they learn. Fortunately, teachers can leverage different motivations, unique to individual students, to help them work toward common sets of learning.

Motivation includes four types of behavior from learners: how they initiate learning, the directions they pursue, the intensity of their work, and their ability to persist in learning (Good & Lavigne, 2017, p. 217). While it can be easy to think of motivation as a permanent characteristic of a person—there are motivated people and unmotivated people—experience and research tell us that our motivation can vary widely from task to task and situation to situation. The environment that surrounds a student's learning plays a big role in their motivation—so much so that deliberately focusing on improving students' motivation should be considered part and parcel of a student-centered learning environment (Moeller et al., 2012).

 ## HOW RESEARCH EVOLVES

One of the most famous studies on student motivation is the "marshmallow study," conducted by Columbia University's Yuichi Shoda and colleagues in the 1970s. In the original study, researchers put a marshmallow on a table in front of a preschooler, asked the child not to eat it, and left the room. The children were promised two marshmallows if they could follow the rules. Researchers claimed that whether students ate the first marshmallow, and even the amount of time they hesitated before doing so, predicted all sorts of learning outcomes, including learning stamina throughout adolescence and SAT scores in later life (Shoda et al., 1990).

Unfortunately, the popularity of this work and its seemingly obvious conclusion has prevented follow-up studies from being nearly as popular. These studies have called the central finding of the marshmallow study into question. In 2018, a repeated version of the marshmallow study found much smaller impacts, most of which were explained by other circumstances about students (Watts et al., 2018). More notably, in 2012, researchers repeated the marshmallow experiment with one key difference: Before being offered the marshmallow, children first had an interaction with the researcher where the researcher either offered and gave them a reward or

(Continued)

(Continued)

offered the reward but never gave it to them (Kidd et al., 2013). This condition—whether the researcher was initially honest with the child—predicted how long preschoolers would wait to eat the marshmallow to a greater degree than any of the self-control factors identified in the original marshmallow study.

What can be learned from this back-and-forth among academic studies? First, what "research says" changes as new work is conducted. Teachers should never rely on one study as the final word on the best approach for working with students. Second, relationships are critical; what motivates students in completing the marshmallow task appears to have less to do with their innate qualities and more to do with whether they can trust that the goal is one they can achieve and whether they can trust that the adult in control is being honest and open with them.

INDIVIDUAL AND SITUATIONAL INTERESTS

Teachers have the opportunity to engage students through two types of interests: individual interest and situational interest (Good & Lavigne, 2017):

- *Individual interests* include those subjects and tasks that a student consistently gravitates toward—for example, their desire to learn more about cars or to work in small groups.

- *Situational interests* are those triggered in the moment by something eye-catching or inspiring; these are attributes of content or learning activities that teachers can make more interesting by connecting them with students' lives.

Situational interests are often the spark that leads to individual interests. If you have an enduring passion today, it may be because someone in your life once showed you how focusing on that passion could be interesting, fulfilling, or fun, and you had lots of practice doing activities that rewarded your focus on that interest.

The impact of tapping into student interests can be quite powerful. In one influential study, assigning students reading texts related to an area they were interested in and had prior knowledge about increased their ability to recall key ideas and effectively summarize those ideas (Recht & Leslie, 1988). Goals offer opportunities to tap into both individual and situational interests. A student's individual interests can drive the topical focus of an ambitious project and build motivation in turn by inspiring the student to complete a research project on a topic of interest or solve math or science problems that help answer a burning question.

Individual interests can also serve as a catalyst for students to improve their overall skills. With her first-graders, Courtney Pawol engages individual interests in reading instruction by giving students broad choice over the topics they read about. By letting students pick their own books for independent reading, she develops their motivation for the reading process and can start the process of guiding them through a progression of increasingly complex texts in that area of interest. One student with an encyclopedic knowledge of and interest in frogs rapidly improved his reading skills because he was strongly motivated to graduate to upper-level texts about frogs. Through frequent conversations, Courtney carefully provided books that were at the student's reading level and other, more challenging texts that provided the student with opportunities to understand what skills he needed to improve to read them fluently.

The environment teachers establish around student goal setting can be a particularly potent way to build situational interest in learning by connecting that learning with longer-term aspirations. In a set of experiments, Destin and Oyserman (2010) found that eighth-grade students who exhibited a focus on long-term professional goals that required college spent more time on homework, had higher grade point averages, and planned to spend extra time on studying and homework. While students consistently expressed expectations that they would attend college, the goal of pursuing a college-dependent adult identity motivated actual changes in behavior.

More importantly, students' environment played a substantial role in that focus: In one iteration of the Destin and Oyserman experiment, students were randomly sorted into two groups. Those students shown information about certain fields (medicine, business, and law) focused on long-term professional goals more readily than students given information about actors, athletes, and musicians. Students in the first group invested almost eight times more effort in completing an extra credit activity than students in the second group. Put another way, all student participants in the experiment had interests and motivations that could drive their effort. The students who had those interests recognized by their teacher and activated through reflection saw their interests reflected in additional effort.

All students have interests and motivations. For some students, these interests and motivations are regularly identified and acted upon, leading them to build the motivational muscle necessary to persevere through learning challenges and reach aspirational goals. Other students' interests and motivations are ignored, and the students lose that opportunity. What separates these two groups of students is not something inside them—it's what the adults in their lives choose to do, or not to do, to bring those interests to the surface.

REFLECT

Think about the last student who told you about an aspiration: a future career, something they wanted to get better at, or something they wanted to become. For students who haven't yet developed a clear aspiration for their long-term future, consider what skills they want to use independently or what skills they could use to build power for themselves or for those important to them. How could you help this student connect their aspiration to the content at your grade level?

STRATEGIES FOR FINDING RELEVANCE

Goals can support student motivation when they have relevance for learners. The research reviewed here on motivation suggests that relevance can be cultivated for almost any learning activity.

First, students find relevance in goals that include learning tasks that relate to their preexisting interests. Connecting to students' interests can help them perform better by allowing them to tap into the knowledge they already possess about a subject.

Second, students find relevance where an educator has helped them connect the goal or its tasks with situational motivations. Many of these motivations relate to universal desires: to be heard, to succeed at what we try, or to be helpful to others. Effective educators show students how specific academic skills can be used in daily life and how understanding the narratives of literature or history can help us understand the worlds in which we live (Good & Lavigne, 2017).

Finally, strategies that build relevance often take place in large-group settings in which students can see the success of their peers and feed off each other's motivations (Good & Lavigne, 2017). Ensuring that students understand how and where others find relevance in their own goals builds a set of cultural expectations around the joy and fulfillment that comes from learning, increasing the likelihood that students will draw situational motivation from pursuing learning for its own sake.

USING INTENTIONS TO BUILD PERSONAL RELEVANCE

Though students' motivations play a central role in helping them understand the relevance of a learning activity, those motivations aren't always apparent to their teacher or even to the students themselves. Part of the developmental process of learning how to set goals is learning how to understand the attributes or characteristics that motivate us as individuals: to name them, to describe them, and to put them into practice. Teachers can use structured activities to lead students to those reflections.

Sixth-grade teacher Caryn Miller centers her students' goal-setting practice by reflecting on a personal intention. An intention, she says, is "one simple word that guides you to focus on your intent for that time in your life or the year." Providing a less-structured opportunity for students to reflect on the types of progress that are meaningful to them builds confidence in the process as a whole.

Students start by brainstorming a set of key words that can describe their intention—*confidence, determination, perseverance,* and other positive character attributes. After choosing one of these words and writing a reflection on what the word means to them, students then build their own in-school and out-of-school goals based around that word. "Because it's about the whole child, I want to make sure they're also focusing on themselves outside of school," explains Caryn. Figure 5.1 shows some examples of the short reflections students have written around their words of intention.

Intention helps to frame the students' reflections throughout the goal-setting process. When reflecting on progress in the middle of a goal, Caryn asks students to identify next steps with their word of intention in mind. These reflections include self-assessment prompts: "I work with [my word of intention] and goal in mind and try to achieve it." Including intention in this way brings an added personalized dimension to self-assessment by letting students determine not only how they've made progress but also what values they are making progress toward.

Figure 5.1

My Intent
Success

My word for this year is success. I chose the word success because the word success means trying hard, and focusing, so you can get to your goal. To some people success means winning a sports game or finishing a test early. To me success means making good choices, trying your best, and being fair, civil, and respectful to those who try to help you. Success is given to those who want it.

BRAVE

What word I choose is brave. And the reason is because in your life you're going to have many challenges and you're going to have to be brave. And my second reason is that it is one of my favorite movies. And one last thing is I also just like the word like something about it is I don't know it just pops.

Never Give Up

I chose never give up because it's important to not give up. You are going to make mistakes at first but that doesn't mean you can't complete the test. If you keep trying no matter what and if you believe in yourself you are going to know that you can do it.

Source: NWEA/Caryn Miller

Elevating student intentions also provides students with broader community support for developing as learners. Caryn recalls when a school administrator talked with a student about certain behaviors and invoked the student's intention as a concept to guide how the student should act moving forward. This shared language among student, teacher, administrator, and others creates opportunities for many adults to support students' progress.

Caryn sees these intentions as helping to build persistence throughout the goal-setting process. "As great as it is to set goals with the kids," she says, "we know we don't always meet them. And that can be disappointing or overwhelming." With an intention in place, Caryn leads students through reflecting on how their intention can help motivate them to accomplish a goal and how it can help them adjust goals if they don't succeed at first.

While this overarching intention lasts an entire year, Caryn's students still set goals for themselves every one to two weeks by focusing on short-term learning targets or other measurable nonacademic objectives. Their intention becomes the most important lens to bring to that process, helping them articulate how the goal-setting process is meaningful and letting them choose some of the criteria by which they'll understand their successes.

PLAN

Consider ways of connecting a goal-setting process to other ways you ask students to express their values in the classroom: whether through guided reflection processes focused on social-emotional learning, character education, or other ways in which students describe themselves to one another. Plan a lesson in which you connect these ideas to students' short-term goals. Consider how a student's self-identity might influence how they'll understand whether a goal has been successful.

PROVIDING OPPORTUNITIES FOR STUDENT EXPRESSION

Student motivation and personal relevance often go hand in hand. Not surprisingly, students are more motivated by lessons and activities that are relevant to their lives. Students are equally unmotivated when the link between a lesson and the real world is unclear. This close relationship, however, makes it relatively easy to assume that a task will be motivating if it appears relevant to us. Fully engaging students with personal relevance requires understanding students more deeply and giving them the opportunity to directly make connections for themselves.

The debates over educational technology make this dynamic clear. In the 21st century, technology is clearly essential in helping students connect with one another, understand complex topics, and practice the skills they'll need to succeed as modern citizens. Many of the techniques for virtual instruction teachers learned in the trial-by-fire of the COVID-19 pandemic will continue to be useful for students who can't be in a school building for whatever reason in the years to come. Access to technology in the classroom is a clear issue of student equity: Applying learning in authentic ways requires that students are able to use the kinds of modern tools they'll use in college, in the workplace, and elsewhere.

But too many teachers think simply including a shiny new app in a lesson gives that lesson relevance in and of itself. They may gravitate toward apps because of the promise of big benefits to engagement from a generation used to working in connected ways. Teachers often trade the names of the new apps they've used without providing the context around how and why those apps were useful. Even worse, administrators may be drawn in by a clever sales pitch or exciting new features. One research organization—the EdTech Evidence Exchange at the University of Virginia—estimates that up to $41 billion is spent on educational technology in the United States each year with little evidence of what tools actually promote learning under which circumstances (Epstein, 2021).

The key to using educational technologies well—in goal setting as in any other kind of instruction—lies in keeping the fundamentals of good teaching and learning the same. Technology does not replace the need for effective educators to help students focus on growth, identify multiple strategies and tools to solve problems, or give students voice and choice over their educational pathways. Instead, it should strategically boost these important priorities, providing additional opportunities for students to see a problem in a new way, get concrete examples of how learning applies to their lives, and express their individual interests and creativity.

A former state teacher of the year, middle grades English Language Arts (ELA) teacher Eric Johnson applies technology to help students understand why goal setting is relevant to them. While he often starts with students using the SMART goal-setting process described in Chapter 3, he looks to quickly move students toward more open-ended descriptions of their goals that require higher-order thinking processes. "The goal doesn't mean much," he says, "if it ends up in a manilla file, shoved away and forgotten about." To keep goals out of that manilla file, students are asked to share their goals—and the frameworks they use to set them—through whatever type of presentation method makes most sense to them.

Figure 5.2

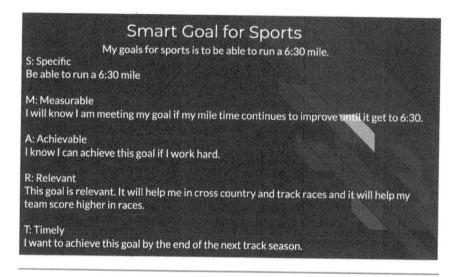

Figure 5.3

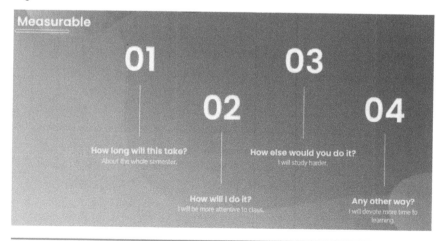

Figure 5.4

Eric makes multiple media available to students to describe how they set goals. Figures 5.2, 5.3, and 5.4 show videos students have used to describe their goals. Eric's students also have the option to use animations, comics, narrations, writing tasks, or other forms of creative expression to describe their goals. Eric reflects,

> Students became invested in the project and loved sharing their curricular, socio-emotional, sports and even fantastic, goals in a manner which best expressed themselves. The scaffolded approach allowed students from diverse backgrounds to work and present at a level that was comfortable for them. A student who struggled with writing and grammar, for instance, created an iMovie showing each acronym and then used images, GIFs and captions to showcase a goal regarding becoming a better reader. Another student who is terrified to read aloud used an electronic text to speech add-on to articulate their goal as it appeared on an interactive slideshow, explaining her goals for soccer training during the pandemic. Another camera-shy student used animated characters to present her goal of meeting and making new friends to her remote-learning peers. . . . The impact on student goal setting was profound as students were excited to create and present and were very responsive when viewing and commenting on one another's objectives.

Giving students access to digital tools (for example, PowerPoint, video creation, and other forms of multimedia) allows students to put emotional energy into their goals and use their favorite tools of creative expression as an individual motivator in the process. Saving these share outs provides the added benefit of drawing out shy students and sharing the most exciting approaches across class periods.

Two additional guidelines make this process easier. First, Eric does not restrict students to goals in ELA; in fact, he generally finds that students who set athletic, social, or other types of goals have an easier time transferring their skill set into academic goals when the time is right. You can let students know that there are a lot of ways they can set goals, ways goals can be organized, and ways to know when you've achieved them. Second, a critical prerequisite to creative goal sharing is creating an emotionally and intellectually safe environment in which students feel comfortable expressing themselves. While students sharing goals with each other is an important part of his process, it can be inauthentic or even hurtful to students if they aren't yet ready to share personal details with each other.

Eric's strategy creates relevance for students in three ways. First, by getting the opportunity to use their own creative outlets, he taps into individual motivators that are already important in students' lives. This approach can help to quickly dispel the idea that goal setting is not for students who are less comfortable with a more linear approach. Second, by having students share with each other, he provides his classes with powerful peer testimonies of the impacts that setting goals have had on their lives. Building these examples proved an engaging high-order task for higher-achieving students and helped break down some of the potential social barriers between higher-achieving students and lower-achieving students. Finally, the work Eric asks students to do taps into their deeper motivations for setting goals in the first place: the types of things they want to achieve and the people they want to become. Students can more easily see themselves in their goals because they've had the opportunity to literally depict themselves in a graphic, cartoon, or video.

There is no magic app. Many of the ideas presented throughout this book could be applied completely using pen-and-paper techniques. In Eric's case, many of the kinds of office productivity and media production tools he asks students to use have been around for a long time. Instead, Eric uses technology as another tool in the classroom to support different forms of student expression. The activities he's designed allow students to seek meaning in the goal-setting process for themselves, then share what they've learned with their peers.

> *Creating engaging classwork using technology requires more than putting a device in front of students.*

Creating engaging classwork using technology requires more than putting a device in front of students. Focus instead on creating opportunities for students to find and express their own motivations, using the tools to add richness to expressing what their goals mean to them rather than as a stand-in for that expression and choice.

ACT

While strategies for finding the relevance behind learning can take many forms, they often begin with opportunities for students to share their own individual motivators with each other and learn from each other's experiences. Design a whole-class exercise to allow students to develop and share their own motivations. Find appropriate ways to set the conversation in motion (a video, a guiding activity, or some other artifact or process that focuses students on their motivations for learning), but make sure to give the students center stage.

UNEARTHING THE MEANING BEHIND LEARNING

The old methods of creating relevance—speaking in general terms to the value of literacy or mathematics in adult life—simply aren't personal enough to reach learners where they are. While a poster showing a celebrity happily reading a book may grab a few students' attention, or a list of jobs that use math skills might initially pique some students' interest, these types of images can't show why reading a specific text, engaging in specific forms of math practice, or mastering a particular set of content can help students become the kinds of people they want to become. These types of general messaging strategies make for great classroom décor; they are less effective at creating the meaningful persistence through difficult academic tasks that a true sense of relevance brings.

In hindsight, as adults, it is relatively easy to connect our education to the aspirations we had for our lives. Students have a trickier task. The purpose of learning on any particular day is always present, but it's also often buried and intangible. Students need a guide, one with deep knowledge of the ins and outs of their academic content who also brings the kind of inquiring mind that can help them uncover their ambitions and tie those together with a string of learning targets and success criteria. Whether through a low-tech or a high-tech process, teachers can help students see relevance and intrinsic value in learning by creating spaces for students to express what their goals mean to them. The short-term academic goals that follow are grounded in these motivations, ensuring that students understand why working toward their goals matters for what they want to achieve and who they want to become.

But making decisions *for* students is a very different mindset and approach than *guiding* them. The next chapter addresses a theme interwoven throughout the process of goal setting that is central to the success of any goal: giving students the freedom to choose. This freedom requires that teachers be willing to give up some of their authority over students' learning paths. Instead, teachers must engage in the complex and intricate work of helping students find meaning in what they've chosen. While that work is likely more challenging, it is also more rewarding; it builds classrooms where students are developed and empowered as learners.

CHAPTER SUMMARY

▶ All students bring their own set of aspirations that learning can help them achieve. Research on what motivates students shows that motivation changes based on the environment students are in, the supports they're given by adults, and the successes they see among their peers.

▶ Two main types of motivators are individual interests (things we're routinely interested in) and situational interests (things that someone shows us are relevant to us). Effective goals tap into both motivators.

▶ Focusing on students' intentions—long-term themes for their academic and nonacademic lives—can help them to find meaning in their goals and build support for them to achieve those goals.

▶ Educational technology provides useful opportunities for students to express their own motivations in different ways, as long as the activities using technology are carefully designed and you avoid adopting a new tool for its own sake.

USE STUDENT CHOICE TO SUPPORT AUTONOMY

6

No matter how much you personally enjoyed and valued learning as a student, there were still probably days you didn't want to go to school. As institutions, schools aren't designed to produce eager participation from students. We ask students to wake up early—often earlier than is ideal for their physiology (Owens et al., 2010)—sit for long periods in a classroom with relatively little physical activity, and learn content in a set order they can't change. Even in a perfect world, not all classroom activities would be inherently interesting or motivating: As everywhere else in life, classrooms have rules to follow and repetitive tasks that must get done (Reeve, 2009). Because school attendance is required by law, no student's participation can ever be said to be truly voluntary (Dörnyei, 2001). Given a real choice, some students would opt out of school entirely: For them, the design of traditional school drains motivation.

However, it would be a tragic error to confuse this lack of motivation for *schooling* with a lack of motivation for *learning*. Aristotle believed the desire to acquire knowledge was an inherent quality of human beings. Parents of young children know what it's like to hear endless questions about the ways the world works. Most teachers can personally attest to the allure and draw of learning for students who understand the connection between what they are learning and the world around them. Even those ostensibly dull or uncompelling tasks can become exciting when students have the opportunity to frame them within the context of their broader goals or needs; students can choose not to be bored if they understand how completing a task gets them closer to what they want (Reeve, 2009). What's the secret, then, to motivating kids to engage in learning (and in school)? Provide supports that enhance student autonomy.

When I spoke to sixth-grade teacher Lindsay Deacon, she said it directly: "When you set a goal for somebody else, that's your goal. That's not their goal." For goal setting to be authentic, students must be provided with multiple opportunities to make choices and exercise freedoms. That means more than letting students craft goals in their own language; it means ultimately giving students authority and responsibility over what their goals are, how they will achieve them, and how they will monitor their success. This level of autonomy can be intimidating because it feels like letting go of control: We can imagine the chaos that might result! However, with adequate foundations in place—such as clear learning targets, goal-setting routines and norms, frequent check-ins, and a classroom environment in which students feel valued—student autonomy will enhance engagement and motivation to learn.

Goal setting provides a mechanism to connect a student's inherent motivation to learn with the day-to-day activities that happen in school. As discussed in the last chapter, helping students find relevant goals is half of that connection; students are more likely to decide to engage if they believe the content of a learning task matters to them. But just as students must engage with the *content* of learning, students should also feel that they're part of a learning *process* in which they exercise meaningful control and influence. Once that relevance is established for students, one of the clearest and most powerful instructional steps teachers can take is letting students themselves take control of what and how they learn while still keeping learning at the center.

> No matter how your classroom is designed or how much authority you exercise over students, they always retain the most important decision: the choice to engage in learning.

No matter how your classroom is designed or how much authority you exercise over students, they always retain the most important decision: the choice to engage in learning. Ultimately, students decide whether or not to engage based on the environment around them and the attitudes and beliefs of themselves, their peers, and their teachers. Teachers support that decision by providing an environment in which those student choices are valued and respected. By allowing student autonomy to flourish in an organized and meaningful way, teachers can tap into powerful motivational forces for learning that are ultimately more powerful than just about any other instructional decision they make (Brookhart et al., 2009).

THE EMOTIONS BEHIND MOTIVATION

The literature on mastery and performance orientation summarized in Chapter 1 is one way of categorizing the kinds of motivations students have. That literature, as well as most other major theories of motivation, places central importance on the role of emotions (Seifert, 2004). How students feel about what they're learning controls how they will think about learning and how they think about learning means a great deal to their success in learning.

What unites strong mastery orientations is a sense of self-efficacy and self-control (Seifert, 2004). *Self-efficacy* is students' confidence in their own capabilities, what they believe they can do. *Self-control* is the extent to which students believe they can affect their success—a student's ability to have autonomy over their own actions, rather than their compliance with someone else's choices. Mastery-oriented students, in other words, believe that they can learn at a high level and that they are in control of that learning.

Self-efficacy and self-control (and other similar terms) can sometimes incorrectly suggest something unchanging about students that determines their success or failure. In actuality, research repeatedly shows self-efficacy, self-control, and other characteristics of effective engagement change and develop based on a student's learning environment (Sökmen, 2021). Put another way, the trust that comes in a culturally responsive and affirming classroom produces self-efficacy for students, rather than the other way around.

> Building trust isn't about "making students feel good about themselves" but instead is about showing them respect by acknowledging their personhood and lived experiences.

Too often, caring for students' emotional well-being is assumed to be the opposite of focusing on rigorous, high-quality instruction. This false choice neglects the extensive research on the relationship among student well-being, the brain, and the ability of students to learn. Hammond's (2014) *Culturally Responsive Teaching and the Brain* focuses on the importance of building trust with students precisely so they can best learn. Building trust isn't about "making students feel good about themselves" but instead is about showing them respect by acknowledging their personhood and lived experiences, particularly the inequities that impact disadvantaged students and students of color. There are many ways to generate trust with students; Figure 6.1 describes five "trust generators" you can use in the

Figure 6.1 Trust Generators

What It Is	What It Looks Like in General	What It Can Look Like in Goal Setting
Selective Vulnerability	Sharing your own challenges as a student or as an adult	Showcasing your own goals, how you achieve them, and how you overcome setbacks
Familiarity	Interacting with students socially inside and outside of school	Attending extracurricular activities where students showcase their talents and using these as examples of good goals
Similarity of Interests	Sharing similar hobbies, sports, social causes, and the like	Pointing to famous athletes, artists, or activists and showing how they meet their own goals
Concern	Remembering specifics about a student's life and asking them questions	Considering how family members and friends can support students in meeting their goals
Competence	Using your own skills and knowledge to show a willingness to support learning	Coming to goal-setting sessions prepared, with several resources and strong knowledge of academic content and progressions of learning

Adapted from Hammond (2014).

classroom. Once trust is in place, Hammond emphasizes, it frees up the brain to focus on creativity, learning, and higher-order thinking.

Self-efficacy comes from the opportunities students have to experience success in mastering content and the way teachers and peers talk about that success (Usher & Pajares, 2008). Consider the choices that can be made available to students in a typical lesson. In fourth grade, an important Common Core standard in speaking and listening (SL4.4) asks students to report on a text, tell a story, or recount an experience using appropriate facts and descriptive details. Meeting this standard by asking each student to give a report on the same book, for example, would miss a valuable opportunity to build trust by letting students connect their own preferences and experiences to academic success. But a teacher can instead let students tell the stories *they* want to tell: the kinds of literature they connect with or real-life anecdotes with their own rich characters and details. Students' experiences in learning this standard hinge on whether they're given the opportunity to choose to tell those stories, whether they have the trust in their teacher to know those stories will be affirmed and validated, and whether their teacher and their peers value hearing those stories.

When setting goals with students, it may be most important to simply remember the role emotions play in how students understand their learning and think about next steps. A student obsessed with avoiding failure, for example, is often less concerned about failure itself than about avoiding "the *implication* of failure, namely inability" (Seifert, 2004, p. 141). By being able to identify and name these emotional pitfalls, teachers can help students manage them and ultimately increase the likelihood that students will be successful in attaining their goals.

Self-efficacy and self-control are powerful stuff. These twin emotions make themselves known through powerful emotions, "feelings of helplessness, hopefulness, pride, [and] guilt" (Seifert, 2004, p. 145). Classrooms provide the resources that teachers can help use to identify those emotions and channel them in the positive directions that support learning. What students seek in a classroom is shared control: the ability to make decisions, interact with peers, and express their opinions (Sökmen, 2021). In order to develop social-emotional skills and mindsets, in other words, teachers should begin by creating the learning routines, expectations, and attitudes that give students the time and opportunities to build their own autonomy and to exercise that autonomy by making choices.

THE RESEARCH ON STUDENT AUTONOMY

Building autonomy for students is a long-term aim of all education. Autonomy is "the ability to take responsibility for one's learning" (Moeller et al., 2012, p. 154): to independently engage in learning tasks, assess performance, and understand next steps. As with all the other social-emotional skills described in this book, autonomy is not innate but instead develops through practice inside and outside the classroom. Teachers can act as a guide by providing activities and opportunities that give students practice with increasing degrees of autonomy over time.

Despite well-documented evidence of the impact of supporting student autonomy in learning—that it improves grades, task performance, creativity, self-worth, and other indicators of student well-being—trained observers find that most teachers employ controlling behaviors rather than autonomy-supportive ones (Reeve, 2009). Teachers do this, Reeve argues, for a variety of reasons, including their inherently powerful social role, the value our culture places on control, and as a reaction to student passivity and disinterest.

There are lots of learning tasks students don't get choice over. Being supportive of autonomy does not mean letting students opt out of learning essential standards, decide not to engage in certain activities (for example, independent reading), or skip doing their homework. Autonomy-supportive teachers instead provide structure for these activities by first taking the student's perspective ("I know you don't want to do this right now") and then providing rationale for the activity ("but here's why reading is so important in this classroom"). This strategy helps students connect the activity with the situational interests discussed in Chapter 5: using learning to reach universal aspirations (skillfulness, success, or control).

Whether the pressure to exert more control over the classroom comes from administrators, students, or from teachers themselves, being aware of this natural tendency is the first step toward counteracting it. Reeve encourages teachers to become more autonomy supportive by consciously attending to their sentiments, language, and behaviors to avoid those that imply or lead to more controlling attitudes. By replacing these with well-justified autonomy-supportive behaviors, teachers can begin to inspire students to be more motivated in their classroom environment.

In one interesting experiment in which teachers were observed helping students solve a set of logic puzzles, Reeve and Jang (2006) classified teachers' behaviors as supporting or discouraging student autonomy and then measured students' interest, enjoyment, and success in solving the puzzles. Using this data, they identified eight autonomy-supporting behaviors that had positive impacts on student outcomes (see Figure 6.2). Six behaviors associated with controlling students' behavior hurt their overall results, including giving students the answer, giving them commands, and telling the student they should do something. Even when working on the same learning target, teachers have the opportunity to influence how well students perform through words and actions that give students permission to solve problems their own way and praise them for doing so.

Goal-setting processes can include each of these eight positive behaviors. Goal-setting conversations focus on creating time for student-teacher interactions, encouraging effort, and offering progress-enabling supports. Goals direct students toward independent work that provides opportunities to demonstrate improvement and mastery. A goal-setting experience that prioritizes student choice leans heavily on students' perceptions, experiences, and preferences. Certainly, goal setting is not the only instructional strategy that

Figure 6.2 Behaviors That Support Student Autonomy

Practice	What It Looks Like in General	What It Can Look Like in Goal Setting
Spend time listening	Paying full attention to the student, shown verbally and through nonverbal cues	Attending to goal-setting conferences as an active listener
Create time for independent work	Providing time for students to solve problems in their own ways	Giving students independent time for goal planning or goal reflection before conferring with them
Give students opportunities to talk	Giving space for students to express themselves	Making sure students do most of the talking when planning for or reflecting on goals
Praise signs of improvement and mastery	Frequently communicating positive feedback—"Good job" or "That's great"	Providing positive reinforcement when students complete goals
Encourage students' efforts	Frequently encouraging student persistence—"You're close" or "You can do it"	Reminding students of their hard work and previous successes when processing goals
Offer progress-enabling hints	When students are stuck, reminding them what has worked in the past or suggesting a strategy that might make solving the puzzle easier	Asking students to reflect on barriers to their success and brainstorming ways to overcome those barriers
Respond to questions and comments	Using replies to student questions and comments to affirm that they are making progress and encourage their persistence through positive phrases—"You have a good point" or "Right"	Showing you support the choices students make in their goal processes through words and actions
Acknowledge students' experiences	Showing empathy through students' perspectives and standpoints—"I know this is a sort of difficult one"	Acknowledging that goals are meant to be challenging but that challenging goals are satisfying

supports these behaviors. However, the relationship between goal setting and improved student outcomes in some studies is likely due in part to how it brings these behaviors together in a single, systematic approach.

What's more, younger and older students alike benefit from structures that give them as much choice as can support learning while also providing empathy and rationale for activities where choice is not possible.

CREATING OPPORTUNITIES FOR AUTHENTIC CHOICES

Supporting student autonomy in setting goals doesn't mean taking a hands-off approach to those goals. Teaching interventions are key to creating an environment in which students can make authentic choices that lead to motivated learning. One way to understand the need for teachers to intervene comes from the difference between *picking* and *choosing*. *Picking*, in this case, means making a selection without considering your own desires or preferences. *Choosing* means acting on those desires and preferences in meaningful ways (Ullmann-Margalit & Morgenbesser, 1977).

When student autonomy doesn't have strong impact, it may be because students are picking instead of choosing (Katz & Assor, 2007). In one study highlighted by Katz and Assor, for example, students were provided a "choice" between activity packets without knowing what the packets actually contained. In other studies, students were given multiple options for what to learn, but they found none of the options particularly interesting. Students may also be picking instead of choosing when a teacher's preference for one option over another is clear or when one option is obviously more rigorous or difficult. Authentic choices require that students select an option based on their own preferences, without focusing on minimizing the risk of failure or pleasing authority figures. Teachers build the context in which those authentic choices take place.

Katz and Assor (2007) identify three key characteristics of authentic classroom choices:

1. **Choice should be relevant to students' interests,** supporting their need for autonomy. Here, note that the quality of choices matters more than the quantity of choices: Students are more engaged with a few choices that are relevant to

them than with several sets of irrelevant choices. (Strategies to build relevance in student goals are discussed in depth in Chapter 5.)

2. **Choices should not be too numerous or overly complex.** With too many choices, students fall back on strategies for navigating the choices rather than acting on preference. They can also become so overwhelmed with choice that they opt out of making a choice entirely, picking at random or ceding the choice back to the teacher.

3. **Choices must fulfill students' need for relatedness.** Students want to feel that their learning parallels the work of the rest of the class, even if they have the ability to move independently through that learning.

Even where student autonomy is high, students should continue toward a common set of learning objectives and outcomes. Many teachers make the error of setting an overarching learning goal for a class and expecting students to adapt that goal to their own needs without providing structured supports (Dean et al., 2012). Paradoxically, this strategy might end up actually reducing students' autonomy: If students are unable to set a learning goal for themselves, the class goal set by a teacher will instead take its place and squeeze student choice out of the equation. If students' goals are unrelated to mastery of the course content, they may be unable to understand or accept that overarching learning objective (Dörnyei, 2001).

Many kinds of choices can have a positive impact on learning, as long as the learner experiences their choice as meaningful (Katz & Assor, 2007). Students can be drawn to two main types of choices (Good & Lavigne, 2017): *action choices* and *option choices*. Action choices relate to how students spend their time; for instance, whether they practice skills individually or in a small group. Option choices focus on which problems, content areas, or other topics to address next. Different types of choices are more or less rewarding for different students, but there is often the flexibility even within a strict scope and sequence to allow students at least one of these two options. Even when working on something as straightforward as practicing for a quiz in spelling or arithmetic, students can be given the chance to choose whether to practice by themselves or with a group game, and they can be asked to identify the specific words or math facts they need to focus most of their time on.

Goal setting offers several opportunities to make choices: Students can choose what their goal is, the steps they will take to accomplish their goals, the means by which they'll practice a skill, and the approach they will take to understanding and assessing their performance. These options provide the opportunity to gradually release responsibility to beginning goal setters, providing one or two options in the beginning and moving toward students exercising choice over the entire process. By engaging with a goal-setting process in a collaborative way, effective teachers can help strike the careful balance between too little autonomy and too few constraints.

PREPARING FOR CHOICES IN ADULT LIFE

In addition to supporting deep learning, building student autonomy through goal setting also helps prepare students for full participation in adult life. As an expert in STEM (science, technology, engineering, and mathematics) education in his district, Matthew Marchyok has had ample opportunities to consider how choice and empowerment support students as they transition to adult life. Part of the role of modern schooling, he argues, is preparing students for a working world in which occupations change frequently, and students will be asked to reinvent their skills and dispositions along with those changes: "With kids, asking them to 'reinvent yourself'—that's way too abstract." Goal setting instead serves as concrete practice in evaluating a problem and reconfiguring your approach to solving it.

Matthew builds ample opportunities for reflection into his classroom processes to help students elevate their own perspectives. "Whatever the questions, you're allowing time, you're allowing space. If they need prompting, you're not jumping in quickly to provide that. You're allowing think time," he explained to me. In open-ended conversations, teachers also provide students with the flexibility to think through and process one of their aspirations, even if the connection to a particular goal isn't immediately obvious.

Matthew believes as a core principle that "students want to be a part of that classroom and see that classroom succeed." To advance the class learning objectives, students bring their own abilities, strengths, and interests. Given the opportunity, they will absorb those traits into their goals and become deeply invested in using those traits to both drive their own learning and support the learning of all their peers.

REFLECT

Return to the goal-setting worksheets provided in Figures 3.1-3.7 of Chapter 3. As you review each one, put a star next to all the places where students could be offered opportunities to make meaningful choices. Identify ways you could use the worksheets over time to gradually release more choice to students, starting with one or two choices and increasing until students are the primary drivers of the conversation.

USING SELF-ASSESSMENT TO SUPPORT AUTONOMY

One critical choice made by learners is deciding how high-quality learning should look. Whether or not students' choices in this area are valued, they're always happening; during and after any learning activity, we all have some sense of how we're performing on that activity relative to our expectations and, often, relative to the work of our peers. These perceptions are significant: Research on self-assessment has regularly found a link between how students self-assess and different motivational outcomes (Yan et al., 2020). Intuitively, what we think of our performance on particular activities adds up into an overall perception of who we are as learners.

By knowing that these habits of mind are consistently human, the practice of self-assessment provides the opportunity for teachers to document those ideas and reinforce to students that their perceptions have value. Through structured self-assessment activities, teachers can get information on what their students think about their own abilities and have the chance to direct those perceptions to ensure that they boost motivation and help students work toward important learning targets. As Lindsay Deacon describes, self-assessment changes the conversation around learning targets: Instead of "slapping those targets on the wall," teacher and students engage in a conversation around how students are interacting with their learning targets.

There are many strategies for self-assessment, ranging in level of documentation and sophistication. At their most basic, teachers can ask students to rate their understanding of the current material during a lesson by using a **visual signal** such as a finger-based scale, a green-yellow-red traffic light, or a thumbs up/middle/thumbs down. With quick cues from the teacher for how students should act on their response, these strategies allow teachers to quickly discover gaps in confidence and address them to keep the class moving at a consistent pace.

Teachers can also design self-assessments that provide specific time and space for students to reflect on their learning. These can vary from highly structured and assignment-specific reflections (a worksheet that asks students to rate how much they know about a standard) to more open-ended opportunities to reflect and act (keeping a journal during a major unit so that students can regularly reflect on their progress). As always, what is most appropriate will depend on the age of the students, their current level of independence, and the specific features of the learning activity. However, teachers who are successful with self-assessment practice can expect their students to move from more-structured to less-structured self-assessments over time.

Self-assessment diaries have been associated with improvements in students' achievement, self-efficacy, and sense of the intrinsic value of a learning activity (Yan et al., 2020). In the study by Yan and coauthors, students were asked to document their current assignment, the criteria they used to self-assess that assignment, and their self-ratings. They were also asked to reflect on their strengths and weaknesses, propose potential future improvements, and report other self-assessment strategies they used throughout the week. Over as little as a five-week period, these 10- to 15-minute diary tasks showed measurable positive effects for students.

Learning portfolios, in which students compile evidence of their learning over a long period, have similar impacts on student achievement and self-efficacy (Belgrad, 2013). In essence, most learning portfolios are versions of a self-assessment diary over a longer period: They combine student work, student reflections on work, and teacher feedback together into a single digestible document. By putting teacher feedback and self-assessment side by side, portfolios may invite students to compare these sources of information against one another, helping teacher and student better coordinate the student's movement toward the objectives of a particular set of learning.

The diary and portfolio tasks have similarities to the tasks described in the tools provided in Chapter 3 for effective goal-setting conversations. That's no accident. Goal setting and self-assessment have a highly complementary relationship, to the point where they may seem indistinguishable from one another. No matter which conceptualization works best for you, the most important takeaway is understanding how allowing students to reflect on their learning in systematic ways contributes to their ability to make independent plans to reach new goals over time.

Students are often some of their own worst critics. In the conversations for this book, several teachers told me about students who had deeply internalized a mistake on a particular assignment or a writing product they felt wasn't up to standard. Even worse, these are often some of their fastest-growing students, who may ignore multiple successes to focus on one perceived misstep. Left uncontrolled, these types of thoughts can quickly ossify into more global judgments; they become the reasons why students believe they aren't good at reading, math, or another academic subject.

In an unmonitored self-assessment process, there are ample opportunities for students to internalize negative or self-defeating messages about their own performance, limiting both their sense of self-efficacy and their growth. One of the chief benefits of a systematized and documented self-assessment process is the opportunity to head off these negative perceptions. By showing students you value their perceptions while also taking the time to highlight their strengths and successes, you can help them build reflective habits that reinforce their identities as successful learners.

PLAN

Return to the learning pathways you created in the ACT exercise of Chapter 2. Review them and identify opportunities for students to self-assess knowledge of key outcomes. Consider how to document students' perceptions of their learning and ideas for their next steps in ways that support building self-efficacy and persistence.

CREATING STRUCTURE TO BUILD AUTONOMY

I once visited a fourth- and fifth-grade class that relied heavily on regular goal setting. Their homeroom was a repurposed school auditorium. There were no desks; instead, students had a variety of zones they could use depending on whether they were working independently, interacting with a small group, or receiving direct instruction. Some students were sprawled out on couches reading. Others were actively pacing around what used to be the school's stage. Others were huddled in a small group around a whiteboard as their co-teacher walked through solving an algebra equation. To an outsider, it looked a bit chaotic, but every student in that room knew where they were supposed to be and what they were supposed to be doing.

Matthew calls this the workshop model of instruction. Like a workshop, a learning environment can be a place that looks dirty and disorganized at first glance. "Tools are on the shelves, tools are being used, tools are dropped on the ground, there's sawdust everywhere . . . things are changing, and they're not always perfectly manicured." You can expect a classroom in which students engage in all different kinds of work to be less orderly, dirtier, and probably louder than the other classrooms in your building. To teachers used to a more controlling environment, this may look like a place where disciplined learning could never occur. The reality couldn't be further from that assumption.

One of the reasons teachers adopt controlling styles instead of promoting autonomy is the false assumption that control is the same thing as structure. At first glance, it seems that controlling behaviors are structured, while autonomy-supportive behaviors are chaotic (Reeve, 2009). Goal setting proves that this is a misconception. The structures of an effective goal-setting practice laid out here rely on consistent and routine procedures, frequent student-teacher interaction, and an ongoing focus on feedback and results. However, rather than seeking to control students, all of these elements focus on empowering and freeing them.

The structure supporting student freedom is what sets goal setting apart as a uniquely powerful and influential instructional practice. As with most foundational changes, the ripple effects of goal setting can have secondary impacts on every other aspect of your classroom, from where students sit to how they're assessed. But it's within that dirty, chaotic, and loud workshop of learning that students can feel that their successes are truly their own.

ACT

In Chapter 1, you completed an action planning worksheet around your personal goal-setting philosophy, approach, and needs. Return to that worksheet now and identify ways in which your opinions, perspectives, and tactics have shifted while reading this book. Write a to-do list with the preparations you'll need to make to put this revised plan into action in your classroom.

CHAPTER SUMMARY

▶ While all students have innate motivation for *learning*, this may not translate readily to innate motivation for *schooling*. Given the right autonomy supports from teachers, students can take responsibility for their learning in school, increasing their engagement and improving their results.

▶ Goal setting offers several opportunities for students to make authentic choices, as long as teachers provide structures through which those choices are meaningful and allow students to relate to one another.

▶ Self-assessment strategies can grow and develop with students to give them greater autonomy in understanding the outcomes of their learning.

▶ A teaching disposition focused on building trust with students and developing their autonomy provides practice for the type of lifelong learning students will engage in as adults in a rapidly changing modern world.

CONCLUSION

A Vision for the Goal-Setting Classroom

One of my most memorable field trips from elementary school was to Living History Farms, a reenactment-based outdoor museum that was a mainstay field trip activity for all the schools in my hometown. At the museum, alongside representations of the typical farm of 1700 and 1850, was a one-room schoolhouse designed to show what school was like in 1876. As we sat in raw, uncomfortable wooden desks, we were shown how our 19th-century peers were given a single common lesson, regardless of grade level or ability. The schoolmarm would seat students in rank order, based on their ability, and send the lowest performers to the corner to wear the dunce cap. I remember feeling a kind of time-based culture shock: It was jarring to move from the classroom of my time, with its own norms and expectations about how students and teachers related to one another, to the norms and expectations of a completely different time.

Sixth-grade teacher Lindsay Deacon has also seen dramatic shifts in classroom culture, though in a much shorter amount of time. During Lindsay's career, she has gone from teaching to instructional coaching jobs and back three separate times. As we talked, she reflected, "Every time that I return to the students, I feel that I am more of a thought partner with them than I am the directive facilitator." For Lindsay, each job transition has been an opportunity to rethink how she interacts with students and build in the evolving best practices that she has seen as an instructional coach.

As with most other aspects of our society, the pace of change in schooling is faster now than it's ever been—and it's accelerating quickly. In describing how some of the best educators use student goal setting to drive their practice, this book has touched on a number of those important developments, including the rise in short-term formative assessment techniques, new abilities to differentiate and scaffold instruction for individual learners, the increasing importance of student social-emotional learning, and cutting-edge neurocognitive research on student empowerment and choice. Taken all at once, it can appear overwhelming.

Indeed, Lindsay argues, that sense of being overwhelmed happens as much for students experiencing a changing classroom as it does for teachers. "I'm empowering them to be in a slightly uncomfortable space where they probably haven't been very much before, having to make their own choices in what they're going to be learning, how they're going to be learning it, and how they're going to show me what they have learned." This can be unusual for kids who are "used to having a worksheet, a thing that tells them what to learn."

Rather than ignoring that discomfort, it's critical that we acknowledge and even celebrate it. The learning that comes from discomfort is undoubtedly why my teachers saw the classroom of 1876 as a valuable learning tool: We were forced to consider how school had changed since then and why it had changed in the ways it had. As with any new teaching practice, goal setting can be another opportunity to produce a compliance mentality, spinning off its own new set of worksheets and set-in-stone steps that don't really lead to fundamental changes in practice. But it can also be a valuable opportunity to reevaluate the relationship between teacher and student—and in so doing, reimagine what a 21st-century classroom looks like.

SPREADING GOAL SETTING TO TEACHERS AND LEADERS

Reading this book may inspire you to consider how setting goals for yourself can support your growth as a teacher and school leader. The research on goal setting among educators identifies many of the same important factors for success for adults as for students: Educators' goals should be specific, be shared within a community, come with regular feedback, and be aligned with their school's ongoing learning strategy (Meyer et al., 2020). The SMART (Specific, Measurable, Achievable, Relevant, and Timely) goal-setting framework is particularly popular for educators, and resources describing how to leverage the framework for yourself are readily available (Conzemius & Morganti-Fisher, 2012; O'Neill & Conzemius, 2006).

The close alignment between how students set goals and how educators set goals shouldn't be particularly surprising. In any learning community, it takes active learning by all members—including teachers and administrators—to realize the full potential of everyone in the community. Practicing goal setting yourself brings authenticity to your

(Continued)

(Continued)

interactions with students: You can tell them about goals you've set and struggled with and how you were able to persist through them.

Kids are excellent hypocrisy meters. They know when something they've been asked to do is designed merely to keep them busy or is being required by someone in authority because of tradition or outside pressure. As with any other ambitious classroom practice, goal setting can fall flat if students see it as a requirement instead of an activity with purpose. By setting goals yourself, you are not only likely to improve all elements of your practice, you're also able to create conversation starters that draw students into the goal-setting process.

WHAT GOAL SETTING TEACHES ABOUT TEACHING

What Lindsay realized by transitioning in and out of the classroom aligns with what developmental psychologists have long recognized: Much of what we thought we knew about learning is changing. The Introduction illustrated those changes through two compelling summaries offered by the National Academies and the work of researcher John Hattie. Learning, we now know, happens most when students are given the processes and tools they need to be able to solve intellectual problems. Learning also happens within a set of social and cultural contexts that effective educators cannot ignore. Into that new vision of learning comes goal setting. In reviewing the research on effective student goal-setting practices in Chapter 1, we also made connections from broad conceptual ideas of how learning works to specific strategies aligned with the realities of the classroom. We also previewed some of the mindset shifts required of both teachers and students to make those changes.

Chapters 2, 3, and 4 focused on the tools teachers bring to an effective goal-setting process. Effective goal setting can happen with students of any age or at any developmental level, presuming that activities are adjusted for them and that they participate in the process of breaking academic standards into meaningful pieces based on what they're ready to learn next. Frequent one-on-one conversations with students keep their goals front and center and help teachers promote persistence and mastery-oriented attitudes from the outset. Formative and benchmark assessment data work together with goals to put students' achievement and growth in context and to give them aspirational but reasonable targets to hit. The combination of these ingredients helps ensure that goal setting is a meaningful process for students that directly impacts their academic path.

Teachers also empower and enable students to set goals by building relevance and choice. Chapter 5 reviews strategies to build relevant goals for students both by targeting their ongoing interests and by helping to make connections between planned learning and students' future aspirations. Chapter 6 underlines the importance of giving students authentic levels of choice in their goals and suggests ways to appropriately increase student responsibility for goals over time.

Many of the themes of these chapters are present to one degree or another in instructional activities. There are many great ways in instruction to engage students, give them autonomy, build a relationship, or gather valuable assessment data. Each of these activities has its own research base, with its own philosophical origins and its own set of documented positive impacts on student learning. Goal setting is an approach to instruction that integrates several of these activities and values into a set of concrete strategies that tell a clear and coherent story to students about how learning takes place.

> By pulling together a variety of threads from new and emerging research on how students learn, goal-setting practice invites a broader transformation of the acts of teaching and learning.

The "sage on the stage" model—what school looked and felt like to students in 1876 and what it still looks and feels like to many students today—is long overdue for a revamp. Teachers with a goal-setting mindset begin with understanding individual student needs, work directly with students to create plans for learning around those needs, and act as coach and mentor to help students access the learning materials they need to complete those plans. Rather than taking a whole class through the same activities at the same time, goal setting makes it likely that (at least sometimes) students are doing all sorts of different activities in different groups with different areas of focus. By pulling together a variety of threads from new and emerging research on how students learn, goal-setting practice invites a broader transformation of the acts of teaching and learning.

SHEPHERDS OF LEARNING

Instructional coach Erin Whitlock has seen firsthand the ways that implementing student goal setting challenges teachers to think about teaching in new and different ways. Doing goal setting authentically, she told me, requires "turning over individual acts of responsibility and ultimate ownership to the student as much as possible." This process, she acknowledges readily, is a lot of upfront work. But, she argues, investing that time on the front end empowers students, builds self-assessment skills, and creates a positive habit of goal setting that crosses grades.

An ideal goal-setting process, Erin says, moves all of the procedures that are part of good instruction from teacher to student: Students identify their own learning targets, select their own resources, assess themselves and peers, and make plans for next steps. While that can require a lot of change, it also creates "a feeling you can touch of purpose, of excitement for learning." That sense of purpose and excitement can transcend goal setting and find its way into all your other instructional activities.

In this idealized version of schooling, where students are the procedural drivers of learning, is there any role for teachers at all? Erin certainly believes so. As they practice lifelong learning skills, students still need "the wisdom, experience, and knowledge of an adult." But this adult, no longer the primary instructor, becomes more of a shepherd: a guide toward the ultimate destination of learning and a source of emotional support and strength along the way.

Every student needs a great teacher. No amount of technological innovation or structural change will eliminate the need for learning directed by caring, knowledgeable adults. What that learning looks like, however, has shifted greatly over time and will continue to shift as students find themselves in a more complex world with a new set of challenges. Students who can set, monitor, and respond to their own goals have been given the tools and the mental models to thrive in this complexity. The teachers who help them build those skills give them a gift: the gift to learn for themselves.

REFERENCES

Allal, L. (2020). Assessment and the co-regulation of learning in the classroom. *Assessment in Education: Principles, Policy & Practice, 27*(4), 332-349. https://doi.org/10.1080/0969594X.2019.1609411

American Educational Research Association, American Psychological Association, & National Council on Measurement in Education. (2014). *Standards for educational and psychological testing.* American Educational Research Association.

Ames, C. (1992). Classrooms: Goals, structures, and student motivation. *Journal of Educational Psychology, 84*(3), 261-271. https://doi.org/10.1037/0022-0663.84.3.261

Ames, C., & Archer, J. (1988). Achievement goals in the classroom: Students' learning strategies and motivation processes. *Journal of Educational Psychology, 80*(3), 260-267. https://doi.org/10.1037/0022-0663.80.3.260

Anderman, L. H., Andrzejewski, C. E., & Allen, J. (2011). How do teachers support students' motivation and learning in their classrooms? *Teachers College Record, 113*(5), 969-1003. https://www.tcrecord.org/Content.asp?ContentId=16085

Andrade, H. L., & Brookhart, S. M. (2020). Classroom assessment as the co-regulation of learning. *Assessment in Education: Principles, Policy & Practice, 27*(4), 350-372. https://doi.org/10.1080/0969594X.2019.1571992

Belgrad, S. (2013). Portfolios and e-portfolios: Student reflection, self-assessment, and goal setting in the learning process. In J. R. Tomlinson (Ed.), *SAGE handbook of research on classroom assessment* (pp. 331-346). SAGE.

Brookhart, S. M., Moss, C. M., & Long, B. A. (2009). Promoting student ownership of learning through high-impact formative assessment practices. *Journal of MultiDisciplinary Evaluation, 6*(12), 42-67.

Burns, E. C., Martin, A. J., & Collie, R. J. (2018). Adaptability, personal best (PB) goals setting, and gains in students' academic outcomes: A longitudinal examination from a social cognitive perspective. *Contemporary Educational Psychology, 53,* 57-72. https://doi.org/10.1016/j.cedpsych.2018.02.001

Cantor, P., Osher, D., Berg, J., Steyer, L., & Rose, T. (2019). Malleability, plasticity, and individuality: How children learn and develop in context. *Applied Developmental Science, 23*(4), 307-337. https://doi.org/10.1080/10888691.2017.1398649

Cauley, K. M., & McMillan, J. H. (2010). Formative assessment techniques to support student motivation and achievement. *The Clearing House: A Journal of Educational Strategies, Issues and Ideas, 83*(1), 1-6. https://doi.org/10.1080/00098650903267784

Chappuis, J., & Stiggins, R. (2020). *Classroom assessment for student learning* (3rd ed.). Pearson.

Ciani, K. D., Middleton, M. J., Summers, J. J., & Sheldon, K. M. (2010). Buffering against performance classroom goal structures: The importance of autonomy support and classroom community. *Contemporary Educational Psychology, 35*(1), 88-99. https://doi.org/10.1016/j.cedpsych.2009.11.001

Collie, R. J., Martin, A. J., Papworth, B., & Ginns, P. (2016). Students' interpersonal relationships, personal best (PB) goals, and academic engagement. *Learning and Individual Differences, 45*, 65-76. https://doi.org/10.1016/j.lindif.2015.12.002

Conzemius, A., & Morganti-Fisher, T. (2012). *More than a SMART goal: Staying focused on student learning.* Solution Tree Press.

Dean, C. B., Hubbell, E. R., Pitler, H., & Stone, B. J. (2012). *Classroom instruction that works: Research-based strategies for increasing student achievement.* ASCD.

DeShon, R. P., & Gillespie, J. Z. (2005). A motivated action theory account of goal orientation. *Journal of Applied Psychology, 90*(6), 1096-1127. https://doi.org/10.1037/0021-9010.90.6.1096

Destin, M., & Oyserman, D. (2010). Incentivizing education: Seeing schoolwork as an investment, not a chore. *Journal of Experimental Social Psychology, 46*(5), 846-849. https://doi.org/10.1016/j.jesp.2010.04.004

Dörnyei, Z. (2001). *Motivational strategies in the language classroom.* Cambridge University Press.

Dweck, C. (2008). *Mindset: The new psychology of success.* Random House.

Dweck, C. (2015, September 23). Carol Dweck revisits the "growth mindset." *Education Week.* https://www.edweek.org/leadership/opinion-carol-dweck-revisits-the-growth-mindset/2015/09

Elliott, E. S., & Dweck, C. S. (1988). Goals: An approach to motivation and achievement. *Journal of Personality and Social Psychology, 54*(1), 5-12. https://doi.org/10.1037/0022-3514.54.1.5

Epstein, B. (2021, March 30). U.S. spends more than $25 billion per year on education technology, new research finds. https://edprepmatters.net/2021/03/u-s-spends-more-than-25-billion-per-year-on-education-technology-new-research-finds/

Formative Assessment for Students and Teachers State Collaborative on Assessment and Student Standards (FAST SCASS). (2018). *Revising the definition of formative assessment.* https://www.ccsso.org/sites/default/files/2018-06/Revising%20the%20Definition%20of%20Formative%20Assessment.pdf

Giddens, L., Leidner, D., & Gonzalez, E. (2017). *The role of Fitbits in corporate wellness programs: Does step count matter?* http://hdl.handle.net/10125/41596

Good, T. L., & Lavigne, A. (2017). *Looking in classrooms.* Routledge.

Gould, S. J. (1994, November 24). Curveball. *The New Yorker.* https://chance.dartmouth.edu/course/topics/curveball.html

Hammond, Z. (2014). *Culturally responsive teaching and the brain: Promoting authentic engagement and rigor among culturally and linguistically diverse students.* Corwin Press.

Hattie, J. (2013). *Visible learning.* Corwin. https://doi.org/10.4324/9780203887332

Hattie, J. (2021). *Visible Learning MetaX* [Data set]. https://www.visiblelearningmetax.com/

Heritage, M. (2010). *Formative assessment: Making it happen in the classroom.* Corwin.

Heritage, M., & Wylie, E. C. (2020). *Formative assessment in the disciplines.* Harvard Education Publishing Group.

Herrnstein, R. J., & Murray, C. A. (1994). *The bell curve: Intelligence and class structure in American life.* Free Press.

Holt, C. (2020, January 22). *5 tips for engaging K-3 students in your responsive planning process.* NWEA Teach. Learn. Grow. Blog. https://www.nwea.org/blog/2020/5-tips-for-engaging-k-3-students-in-your-responsive-planning-process/

Husman, J., & Lens, W. (1999). The role of the future in student motivation. *Educational Psychologist, 34*(2), 113-125. https://doi.org/10.1207/s15326985ep3402_4

Jimerson, J. B. (2016). How are we approaching data-informed practice? Development of the survey of data use and professional learning. *Educational Assessment, Evaluation and Accountability, 28,* 61-87. https://doi.org/10.1007/s11092-015-9222-9

Kardon, S. (1996). Review of the book *The bell curve: Intelligence and class structure in American life,* by Richard J. Herrnstein and Charles Murray. *Social Work, 41*(1), 116-117.

Katz, I., & Assor, A. (2007). When choice motivates and when it does not. *Educational Psychology Review, 19,* 429.

Kidd, C., Palmeri, H., & Aslin, R. N. (2013). Rational snacking: Young children's decision-making on the marshmallow task is moderated by beliefs about environmental reliability. *Cognition, 126*(1), 109-114. https://doi.org/10.1016/j.cognition.2012.08.004

Kingston, N., & Nash, B. (2011). Formative assessment: A meta-analysis and a call for research. *Educational Measurement: Issues and Practice, 30*(4), 28-37. https://doi.org/10.1111/j.1745-3992.2011.00220.x

Lee, I.-M., Shiroma, E. J., Kamada, M., Bassett, D. R., Matthews, C. E., & Buring, J. E. (2019). Association of step volume and intensity with all-cause mortality in older women. *JAMA Internal Medicine, 179*(8), 1105-1112. https://doi.org/10.1001/jamainternmed.2019.0899

Leithwood, K., & Sun, J. (2018). Academic culture: A promising mediator of school leaders' influence on student learning. *Journal of Educational Administration, 56*(3), 350-363. https://doi.org/10/fp4z23

Liem, G. A. D., Ginns, P., Martin, A. J., Stone, B., & Herrett, M. (2012). Personal best goals and academic and social functioning: A longitudinal perspective. *Learning and Instruction, 22*(3), 222-230. https://doi.org/10.1016/j.learninstruc.2011.11.003

Maehr, M. L., & Zusho, A. (2009). Achievement goal theory: The past, present, and future. In K. R. Wenzel & A. Wigfield (Eds.), *Handbook of Motivation in School* (pp. 77-104). Routledge.

Makkonen, R., & Jaquet, K. (2020). *The association between teachers' use of formative assessment practices and students' use of self-regulated learning strategies.* Regional Educational Laboratory West at WestEd.

Maldarelli, C. (2020). This epidemiologist proved 10,000 steps is a lie. *Popular Science.* https://www.popsci.com/story/health/10000-steps-evidence-study/

Marsh, J. A., Farrell, C. C., & Bertrand, M. (2014). Trickle-down accountability: How middle school teachers engage students in data use. *Educational Policy, 30*(2), 243-280. https://doi.org/10.1177/0895904814531653

Martin, A. J. (2013). Improving the achievement, motivation, and engagement of students with ADHD: The role of personal best goals and other growth-based approaches. *Australian Journal of Guidance and Counselling, 23*(1), 143-155. https://doi.org/10.1017/jgc.2013.4

Martin, A. J., & Elliot, A. J. (2016). The role of personal best (PB) and dichotomous achievement goals in students' academic motivation and engagement: A longitudinal investigation. *Educational Psychology, 36*(7), 1285-1302. https://doi.org/10.1080/01443410.2015.1093606

Marzano, J. M. (2009). *Designing and teaching learning goals and objectives: Classroom strategies that work.* Marzano Research Laboratory.

McGregor, H. A., & Elliot, A. J. (2002). Achievement goals as predictors of achievement-relevant processes prior to task engagement. *Journal of Educational*

Psychology, 94(2), 381. https://doi.org/ 10.1037/0022-0663.94.2.381

Meyer, F., Bendikson, L., & Le Fevre, D. M. (2020). Leading school improvement through goal-setting: Evidence from New Zealand schools. *Educational Management Administration & Leadership.* Advance online publication. https://doi .org/10.1177/1741143220979711

Moeller, A. J., Theiler, J. M., & Wu, C. (2012). Goal setting and student achievement: A longitudinal study. *Modern Language Journal, 96*(2), 153-169. https://doi .org/10/cw2ct5

National Academies of Sciences, Engineering, and Medicine. (2018). *How people learn II: Learners, contexts, and cultures.* The National Academies Press. https://doi .org/10.17226/24783

National Research Council. (2000). *How people learn.* National Academies Press. https://doi.org/10.17226/9853

Neely, A. (2019, January 15). How to play music in 9/8 [Video]. YouTube. https://www.youtube.com/watch?v =oGN4juGQ-0A

NGSS Lead States. (2013). *Next Generation Science Standards: For States, By States.* The National Academies Press.

O'Neill, J., & Conzemius, A. (2006). *The power of SMART goals.* Solution Tree Press.

Ogle, D. (1986). K-W-L: A teaching model that develops active reading of expository text. *The Reading Teacher, 39,* 564-570.

Owens, J. A., Belon, K., & Moss, P. (2010). Impact of delaying school start time on adolescent sleep, mood, and behavior. *Archives of Pediatrics & Adolescent Medicine, 164*(7), 608-614. https://jama-network.com/journals/jamapediatrics/ article-abstract/383436

Recht, D. R., & Leslie, L. (1988). Effect of prior knowledge on good and poor readers' memory of text. *Journal of Educational Psychology, 80*(1), 16-20. https://psycnet .apa.org/journals/edu/80/1/16

Reeve, J. (2009). Why teachers adopt a controlling motivating style toward students and how they can become more autonomy supportive. *Educational Psychologist, 44*(3), 159-175.

Reeve, J., & Jang, H. (2006). What teachers say and do to support students' autonomy during a learning activity. *Journal of Educational Psychology, 98*(1), 209. https://doi .org/10.1037/0022-0663.98.1.209

Rosenbaum, L. (2019). *Should you really take 10,000 steps a day?* Retrieved October 12, 2020, from https://blog .fitbit.com/should-you-really-take-10000-steps-a-day/

Safer, N., & Fleischman, S. (2005). Research matters: How student progress monitoring improves instruction. *Educational Leadership, 62*(5), 81-83.

Seifert, T. (2004). Understanding student motivation. *Educational Research, 46*(2), 137-149. https://doi.org/10.1080/ 0013188042000222421

Shoda, Y., Mischel, W., & Peake, P. K. (1990). Predicting adolescent cognitive and self-regulatory competencies from preschool delay of gratification: Identifying diagnostic conditions. *Developmental Psychology, 26*(6), 978. https://psycnet .apa.org/record/1991-06927-001

Sisk, V. F., Burgoyne, A. P., Sun, J., Butler, J. L., & Macnamara, B. N. (2018). To what extent and under which circumstances are growth mind-sets important to academic achievement? Two meta-analyses. *Psychological Science, 29*(4), 549-571. https://doi.org/10/gdfhb5

Sökmen, Y. (2021). The role of self-efficacy in the relationship between the learning environment and student engagement. *Educational Studies, 47*(1), 19-37. https:// doi.org/10.1080/03055698.2019.1665986

Spencer, S. J., Logel, C., & Davies, P. G. (2016). Stereotype threat. *Annual Review of Psychology, 67,*

415–437. https://doi.org/10.1146/annurev-psych-073115-103235

Stiggins, R. J. (2002). Assessment crisis: The absence of assessment for learning. *Phi Delta Kappan, 83*(10), 758–765. https://doi.org/10.1177/003172170208301010

Stronge, J. H., & Grant, L. W. (2014). *Student achievement goal setting.* Routledge. https://doi.org/10.4324/9781315854953

Sullivan, A. N., & Lachman, M. E. (2016). Behavior change with fitness technology in sedentary adults: A review of the evidence for increasing physical activity. *Front Public Health, 4,* 289. https://doi.org/10.3389/fpubh.2016.00289

Ullmann-Margalit, E., & Morgenbesser, S. (1977). Picking and choosing. *Social Research, 44*(4), 757–785. https://www.jstor.org/stable/40971175

Usher, A., & Kober, N. (2012). *Student motivation: An overlooked piece of school reform.* https://www.inflexion.org/student-motivation-an-overlooked-piece-of-school-reform/

Usher, E. L., & Pajares, F. (2008). Sources of self-efficacy in school: Critical review of the literature and future directions. *Review of Educational Research, 78*(4), 751–796. https://doi.org//10.3102/0034654308321456

Watts, T. W., Duncan, G. J., & Quan, H. (2018). Revisiting the marshmallow test: A conceptual replication investigating links between early delay of gratification and later outcomes. *Psychological Science, 29*(7), 1159–1177. https://doi.org/10.1177/0956797618761661

White, K., Hohn, R., & Tollefson, N. (1997). Encouraging elementary students to set realistic goals. *Journal of Research in Childhood Education, 12*(1), 48–57. https://doi.org/10.1080/02568549709594715

Wolters, C. A. (2004). Advancing achievement goal theory: Using goal structures and goal orientations to predict students' motivation, cognition, and achievement. *Journal of Educational Psychology, 96*(2), 236–250. https://doi.org/10.1037/0022-0663.96.2.236

Wurmser, Y. (2019). *Wearables 2019: Advanced wearables pick up pace as fitness trackers slow.* eMarketer. https://www.emarketer.com/content/wearables-2019

Yan, Z., Chiu, M. M., & Ko, P. Y. (2020). Effects of self-assessment diaries on academic achievement, self-regulation, and motivation. *Assessment in Education: Principles, Policy & Practice, 27*(5), 562–583. https://doi.org/10.1080/0969594X.2020.1827221

INDEX

Confident Teachers, Inspired Learners

CAROL PELLETIER RADFORD

This vivid and inspirational guide offers educators practical strategies to promote their well-being and balance. Readers will find wisdom for a fulfilling career in education through teachers' stories of resilience, tips for mindful living, and podcast interviews with inspiring teachers and leaders.

JULIE STERN, KRISTA FERRARO, KAYLA DUNCAN, TREVOR ALEO

This step-by-step guide walks educators through the process of identifying curricular goals, establishing assessment targets, and planning curriculum and instruction that facilitates the transfer of learning to new and challenging situations.

STEPAN MEKHITARIAN

Transition back to school by leveraging the best of distance learning and classroom instruction. Learn how to create a blended learning experience that fosters learning, collaboration, and engagement.

SHIRLEY CLARKE

Learning intentions and success criteria expert Shirley Clarke shows how to phrase learning intentions for students, create success criteria to match, and adapt and implement them across disciplines.

To order your copies, visit corwin.com

No matter where you are in your professional journey, Corwin aims to ease the many demands teachers face on a daily basis with accessible strategies that benefit ALL learners. Through research-based, high-quality content, we offer practical guidance on a wide range of topics, including curriculum planning, learning frameworks, classroom design and management, and much more. Our resources are developed by renowned educators and designed for easy implementation in order to provide tangible results for you and your students.

WARREN BERGER, ELISE FOSTER

Written to be both inspirational and practical, *Beautiful Questions in the Classroom* shows educators how they can transform their classrooms into cultures of curiosity.

ERIC M. ANDERMAN

Delve into the what, why, and how of motivation, its effects on learning, and your ability to spark that motivation using practical strategies to improve academic outcomes.

SERENA PARISER, EDWARD F. DEROCHE

Gain time in each day, reduce stress, and improve your classroom learning environment with 35 practical, teacher-proven strategies for managing time and setting personal boundaries.

CATLIN R. TUCKER

Balance With Blended Learning provides teachers with practical strategies to actively engage students in setting goals, monitoring development, reflecting on growth, using feedback, assessing work quality, and communicating their progress with parents.

CORWIN

A SAGE Publishing Company

Helping educators make the greatest impact

CORWIN HAS ONE MISSION: to enhance education through intentional professional learning.

We build long-term relationships with our authors, educators, clients, and associations who partner with us to develop and continuously improve the best evidence-based practices that establish and support lifelong learning.

An enduring mission

Our mission is simple but vast: Partnering to help all kids learn®. We help kids get what they need in the classroom, so they can pursue their passions, shape their future, and realize their potential.